SHAPING PRAYER

Barbara A Scott

Shaping Prayer
Barbara A Scott
© 1996 Methodist Publishing House

ISBN 1 85852 071 1

CONTENTS

Prayers for the Connexion and other organisations

Blessings

Prayers of Praise, Thanksgiving, Confession and Dedication

❧ ❧ ❧

1.

Praise and Thanksgiving:

Eternal God, you are our creator,
    calling us to be a people.

We praise and adore you

Eternal God, you are our Lord,
    calling us to follow you.

We praise and adore you

Eternal God, you are our peace,
    calling us to live in harmony with you.

We praise and adore you

Eternal God, you are our rock,
    . a place of safety against the storms of life.

We praise and adore you

Lord Jesus, you are the Light of the World,
    coming to dispel our darkness.

We praise and adore you

Lord Jesus, you are the Bread of Life,
    offering food that will last.

We praise and adore you

Lord Jesus, you are Living Water,
    quenching our thirst.

We praise and adore you

Lord Jesus, you are the good shepherd,
    coming to guide and direct us.

We praise and adore you

Holy Spirit, you are our comforter,
    coming to encourage us.

We praise and adore you

Holy Spirit, you are our challenger,
   coming to chase away our apathy.

We praise and adore you

Holy Spirit, you are our guide,
   coming to show us the way.

We praise and adore you

Holy Spirit, you are our counsellor,
   helping us through the difficult times.

We praise and adore you

Eternal God, Father, Son and Holy Spirit, you are everything to us, worthy of our praise and adoration. Through Jesus Christ our Lord. **Amen.**

2.

Collect:

Eternal God, we come to worship. We come with our worries, our needs, our wants, our concerns. We come with all that has happened to us this past week. Come to us, Eternal God, in our need and meet with us, that we might offer all that we are to your service. Through Jesus Christ our Lord. **Amen.**

Praise and Thanksgiving:

Eternal God, you are the same, yesterday, today and forever.
You are unchanging
You are our anchor in an uncertain world
You are our safety in a chaotic world
You are the one on whom we rely.

We worship you, we give you thanks and praise

Eternal God, you are the same, yesterday, today and forever.
You are unchanging
You are our rock when the path is rugged
You are our guide when the way is unclear
You are the one we can always turn to.

We worship you, we give you thanks and praise

Eternal God, you are the same, yesterday, today and forever.
You are unchanging
You are our comfort when life is bleak
You are our shepherd when we stumble and fall
You are the one who is always there.

We worship you, we give you thanks and praise

Eternal God, you are the same, yesterday, today and forever.
You are unchanging.

We worship you, we give you thanks and praise, through Jesus Christ our Lord.   Amen.

Confession:

Eternal God, you are the same, yesterday, today and forever.
You are unchanging.
You sent your Son, Jesus, that we might know your forgiveness.
We come to confess our sin, aware of our need of grace.
Here we are, Lord, in faith and penitence,
    knowing you will forgive.
We ask your forgiveness for all that we have thought, said and done this past week that has denied your love, destroyed our relationships with others and damaged our Christian witness.

(*silence*)

Eternal God, you are the same, yesterday, today and forever.
You are unchanging.
Here we are, Lord, knowing that your grace is sufficient.
Here we are, Lord, offering all that we are,
    knowing you accept all who come.
Here we are, Lord, willing to follow where you send.
In Jesus' Name.   **Amen.**

3.

Collect:

Living God, in this time of worship help us to offer all that we are to your service and fill us with a fresh awareness of your sacrificial love for us. Through Jesus Christ our Lord. **Amen**.

Praise and Thanksgiving:

Living God, you are worthy of our thanks and praise.
Yours the power that created the world
Yours the imagination that gave nature its variety and beauty
Yours the love that created each one of us
Yours the grace that sent Jesus for our salvation.

Living Lord Jesus, you are worthy of our thanks and praise.
Yours the power that broke the chains of sin
Yours the imagination that created difference
Yours the love that calls each one of us
Yours the grace that redeems us from sin.

Living Holy Spirit, you are worthy of our thanks and praise.
Yours the power that sustains and renews us
Yours the imagination that gives life to all
Yours the love that comforts and encourages us
Yours the grace that challenges and prods us.

Living God, Father, Son and Holy Spirit
    you are worthy of our thanks and praise.
Yours the power, the imagination, the love and the grace that creates us, calls us onward, renews us and sends us out.
Living God, Father, Son and Holy Spirit we worship and adore you. **Amen**.

Confession:

Living God, bread of life, we confess our inability to follow your
    way of love.
Father God, we deny your love and seek to be our own gods.
Jesus, our Lord, we deny your love
    and seek to be our own saviours.
Spirit of God, we deny your love
    and seek to live by our own power.

Living God, bread of life, we confess our inability to follow your
    way of grace.
Father God, we deny your grace with our greed
    and self-centredness.
Jesus, our Lord, we deny your grace with our anger and fighting
Spirit of God, we deny your grace with our fear and apathy.
Living God, bread of life, we confess our inability to follow your
way of love and grace.
Forgive us, living God, renew us and restore us into a right
relationship with you, through Jesus Christ our Lord.   **Amen**.

4.

Praise:

Eternal God, we your people gather for worship.
You alone are truly worthy of our praise and adoration.
God the Father, we acknowledge your creative power, your
sustaining activity and your love for us.

We worship and adore you

God the Son, Jesus our Lord, we acknowledge your saving power,
your redeeming activity and your love for us.

We worship and adore you

God the Holy Spirit, we acknowledge your guiding power, your
renewing activity and your love for us.

We worship and adore you

Eternal God, Father, Son and Holy Spirit, we acknowledge your
power, your activity in our lives and your love for us.

We worship and adore you

Accept our praise and adoration offered freely in the name of
Jesus Christ.   **Amen**.

Thanksgiving:

Eternal God, we your people gather for worship.
You are the one to whom our thanks are due.
God the Father, for being with us, for encouraging and challenging us, for your steady presence in our lives day by day:

Thank you

God the Son, Jesus our Lord, for your patience and forbearance, for your gracious presence in our lives day by day:

Thank you

God the Holy Spirit, for your empowering and enabling, for your comforting presence in our lives day by day:

Thank you

Eternal God, in the power of the Spirit and in the name of Jesus we give you thanks. **Amen**.

Confession:

Eternal God, we your people gather for worship.
You are the one who can forgive our sin and renew us for service.
Father, Son and Holy Spirit, we confess our hardness of heart toward you and others, our inability to trust in you, our thoughtless words and actions, the things that separate us from you and each other. Forgive us, we pray, and help us to know your renewing presence, that we might learn to follow you more closely and live for you more eagerly.

In Jesus' name we ask it. **Amen**.

5.

Praise:

Creator God, we can know your love; we exalt your name.
Creator God, your activity surprises us; we exalt your name.
Creator God, your tenderness nurtures us; we exalt your name.
Creator God, we gather to worship you; Father, Son and
   Holy Spirit.

Jesus, you are our Lord, coming to us again and again
You redeem us and renew us.
Holy Spirit, you are our guide, comforting and challenging
You fill us and sanctify us.
We exalt your name.

Creator God, known to us in your Son, Jesus,
Lord Jesus, known to us by your Holy Spirit,
Father, Son and Spirit, known to us in so many ways,
We exalt your name.

Glory be to you, Lord God: Father, Son and Spirit, today and
always. **Amen**.

Confession:

Creator God, our actions and words condemn us.
We are erratic, unsteady and doubtful disciples.
We doubt ourselves
We doubt your love
We fool ourselves into believing that we know best.
We convince ourselves that we can handle life in our own
strength.
We deny your love and run from your compassion, afraid.
You have promised to forgive all who turn to you in faith and
trust.
It is in that promise we trust, and confess our sins.
The chosen sins, the deliberate sins, the unwitting sins; we bring
them all to you, Creator God.
Free us from them, and grant us assurance of your forgiveness.
We ask in the name of him who died that we might know
freedom, our Lord Jesus Christ. **Amen**.

6.

Praise:

God, such a small word, and yet you are immense,
filling the universe with evidence of yourself
filling our lives with knowledge of yourself.

We celebrate you, Lord God

God, such a small word, and yet you are astounding,
filling the world with your mercy and grace
filling our lives with meaning and purpose.

We celebrate you, Lord God

God, such a small word, and yet you are amazing,
filling the world with your compassion and gentleness
filling our lives with the wind of your Spirit
filling our lives with the love of your Son, Jesus.

We celebrate you, Lord God

God, such a small word, and yet you are immense, astounding
and amazing.

We celebrate you, Lord God

Through Jesus Christ our Lord. **Amen**.

Confession:

God, such a small word, and yet you are full of compassion for all
your people. Willing to forgive all our sins. Willing always to let
us start again.
We bring our wrongdoing to you, knowing of your compassion.
We fall so often and in so many ways, and yet you continue
always to love us, and we depend on that.

Forgive us, God.

(silence)

God, forgive us, renew us, revive us and restore us.
Through Jesus Christ our Lord. **Amen**.

* * * *

BEGINNING WORSHIP:

7.

God our Father, friend and brother
God our other.
You have known us always.
You have sought us always.
We come to be in your presence.
Forgive us, cleanse us, restore us,
Fill us with yourself,
That we might worship you.
Through Jesus Christ our Lord.
Amen.

8.

Heavenly Father, we gather as your family to worship you.
Help us to worship you in spirit and in truth. Lord, come to
us now and meet our needs, that we might go from this place
renewed and recreated. **Amen**.

9.

Eternal God, you do not change, you come to us again and
again. As we share in worship come to us afresh and give us
the courage to come to you. In Jesus' name we pray. **Amen**.

10.

God of vision, we come to worship. Fill each one of us afresh
with your Holy Spirit. Give to us the gifts and graces we
need as we seek to be obedient to your call on our lives.
Open our hearts and minds to receive what you have to offer
to us this day. Through Jesus Christ, our Lord and Saviour.
Amen.

11.

Loving God, in this time of worship, open our eyes to see you and each other. Open our hearts to love you and each other. Open our hands to do your work and support one another. Fill us that we might truly worship and leave this place better equipped to serve you in the world. For the sake of your Son, Jesus, we ask it. **Amen**.

* * * *

PRAISE:

12.

Almighty God, we respond to your love with our praise.

We praise you, God the Father,
for your creating and sustaining power
for your presence with us
for continuing to call us by name.

We praise you, Jesus our Lord,
for your life, death and resurrection
for continuing to disturb our apathy
for challenging us to be Christ-like.

We praise you, God the Spirit,
for your guidance and comfort
for your stretching of our spiritual sinews
for your insistence in bringing us always to repentance.

We praise you, Almighty God,
Father, Son and Spirit
for calling, disturbing and stretching us.

Almighty God, we respond to your love with our praise,
take our words and our lives and transform them
that we might be a people
of worship and service.

Through Jesus Christ our Lord.
Amen.

13.

Eternal God, Father, Son and Holy Spirit,
we come as your children in praise and adoration.

Father, your love amazes us

Jesus, your love, humbles us

Spirit, your love washes over us

Father, Son and Spirit, your love empowers us
And in you we find life in all its fullness.

We come with thankful hearts, to praise and worship you,
Receive our praise.
Fill us afresh with a sense of your presence and love
And draw us closer to yourself.

In the name of our Lord and Saviour, Jesus Christ.   **Amen**.

14.

Almighty God, we glorify your name
You are wonderful beyond our imagination
You are powerful and awesome, yet present to us
in the beauty and infinite variety of nature.

We worship you for your greatness
For you have called us by name.
Your hand has guided us
Your grace has sustained us
Your love has won us.

We come to worship and adore.
Through Jesus Christ, our Lord and Saviour.   **Amen**.

* * * *

CONFESSION:

15.

Eternal God, aware of your majesty and power we become aware
of our own sinfulness and our need of your grace.
We confess the sinfulness of so many of our thoughts,
words and actions.
We hurt one another, building walls between ourselves and
other people.
We hurt you, building walls between ourselves and you.
We hurt ourselves, cutting ourselves off from you and
other people.
Forgive us, we pray.
Help us to make amends where we can.
Enable us to accept your forgiveness and move into the future,
knowing that your forgiveness is complete.

Lord God, we dedicate ourselves again to your service. Accept
us, renew us and send us out in the name of our Lord and
Saviour. Jesus Christ. **Amen**.

16.

Lord God, ever present to us
we confess that so often and in so many ways
we fail you and each other.
Too often we go our own way
and deny your love.
We struggle with wants of our own
and you promise to supply our needs.

Lord God, ever present to us
we confess that so often and in so many ways
we selfishly misuse the resources of the world.
Too often we take without giving in return
and deny your grace.
We struggle to be free of your demands
and you promise to equip us for service.

Lord God, ever present to us
forgive us.
Enable us by your Spirit to put failure behind us
and move into the future with you
forgiven and free.

Through Jesus Christ, our Redeemer and friend. **Amen**.

17.

Father, we confess our sinfulness and our need of
    your forgiveness.
We know that when we are truly sorry you are eager to forgive,
    and we come trusting in your mercy.

We confess to you
those things we have done that have denied your love

(*silence*)

those things we have not done that have denied your love

(*silence*)

those things we have said that have denied your love

(*silence*)

those things we have not said that have denied your love

(*silence*)

those things we deliberately chose knowing they denied your love

(*silence*)

those things we were not aware were a denial of your love

(*silence*)

As we contemplate the death and resurrection of our Lord Jesus
    we know that
Learning of you is hard,
    but not as hard as the cross he bore for us.
Obeying you is tough,
    but not as tough as the nails he bore for us.
Following you is pain,
    but not as painful as the thorns he bore for us.
Cleanse us, renew us, restore us, for the sake of your Son,
    who bore so much that we might know freedom.
In the name of Jesus and through the power of the Holy Spirit we
bring this prayer.   **Amen**.

18.

Creator, sustainer
source of all life
dwelling in us,
forgive the times we forget you
forgive the times we deny you
re-create us in the image of your Son
restore our confidence and hope in you.

Spirit of God
refresh each one of us
bring discernment that we might know your way
bring love that we might be channels of your love
bring courage that we might stand firm, proclaiming your healing
love to a broken world.

Through Jesus Christ our Lord. **Amen**.

* * * *

DEDICATION:

19.

God, enlarge our vision of you
increase our faith
give us courage to be open
that your Spirit might move through us
filling us with light and life
enabling us to be your hands in the world. **Amen**.

20.

Father God, we thank you for this time of worship
for your presence and guidance, nurturing and sustaining us.
Be with us as we go from this place of worship
To serve you and each other in our daily lives.
Through Jesus Christ our Lord. **Amen**.

21.

Lord God, fill us afresh with the joy of
knowing you
loving you
following you.
That we might walk eternally in your path. **Amen.**

22.

Father, Son and Spirit
You created each one of us to be unique
You have given to each their gifts.
We stand before you in our uniqueness
In our differences united by your love
In our brokenness healed by your power
In our failure redeemed by your grace
In the reality of our life together
Give us patience to bear with one another
Courage to love one another
and tolerance of one another's failings
That we might be community and live
in peace together.
In Jesus' name we pray. **Amen**.

23.

Lord, you have called us to proclaim your gospel
       in word and deed.
We pray that you will enable us to find ways to·fulfil our calling.
Give us courage as we seek new ways of sharing your gospel.

Lord, you command us to go: let us go in your strength

Feed the hungry. Lord, you have called us to action,
       to be involved in the life of society.
We pray for all people who are feeding the hungry. For all aid
agencies who bring essential food to areas of famine. Give them
patience as they seek to share your love by their actions.

Lord, you command us to go: let us go in your power

Clothe the naked. Lord, you have called us to action, to be involved in the life of society.
We pray for all people who bring clothing and blankets to those in need.
Give them strength as they continue to serve you in serving others.

Lord, you command us to go: let us go in your grace

Heal the sick. Lord, you have called us to action, to be involved in the life of society.
We pray for all people involved in healing work, for doctors, nurses, counsellors and ministers. Give them grace as they seek to bring healing and wholeness.

Lord, you command us to go: let us go in your love

Love the stranger. Lord, you have called us to action, to be involved in the life of society.
We pray for all people who help strangers, we think of the work of the Samaritans, and all who give themselves to listening to and caring for strangers. Give them peace in their work.

Lord, you command us to go: let us go in your Spirit

Visit the prisoner. Lord, you have called us to action, to be involved in the life of society.
We pray for those who visit prisoners, people who give up their spare time, offering friendship and support to those who find themselves on the wrong side of the law. Give them joy as they bring much needed support to others.

Lord, you command us to go: let us go in your grace

Make disciples of all nations. Lord, you have called us to action, to be involved in the life of society.
We pray for all people who work as missionaries overseas.
For people who use their skills in medicine, health care, education, engineering and other work to bring hope to others.
Give them sensitivity to the culture and customs of the people they serve.

Lord, you command us to go: let us go in your power

Lord, you have called us to proclaim your gospel in word and deed. Help us to use our skills in your service, always seeking new ways to fulfil our calling and learning to trust in you more and more. Your Church, the Body of Christ is called to reach out to others; may we take seriously the task of mission, that all people may hear of your love for them.

Lord, you command us to go: let us go in your name

With the power of the Holy Spirit to aid us and with the presence of Jesus Christ to guide us we dedicate ourselves again to your work. **Amen**.

* * * *

OFFERTORY PRAYERS:

24.

Heavenly Father, we bring these gifts freely offered in your service. We pray that you will enable us to use this money wisely as we seek to serve you in this church and circuit. Through Jesus Christ our Lord. **Amen**.

25.

Father God, we are constantly aware of all your gifts to us. We bring these our gifts of money, offering them with love and thanksgiving. Accept these gifts and our thanks through Jesus Christ our Lord. **Amen**.

26.

Eternal God, we bring our gifts of money and ourselves. We pray that you will use both in extending your kingdom in this place. We come in Jesus' name, offering our gifts for his glory. **Amen**.

27.

Almighty God, accept our gifts of money freely offered to you as a token of our love and willingness to serve you. Take these gifts, Lord, and use them and us as you see fit. In Jesus' name and for his sake. **Amen**.

28.

Lord, you have given yourself so freely for us and we come offering ourselves freely to your plan for our lives. We bring our gifts of money, an expression of our commitment, our love and our thanksgiving. Please help us to use this money well that we might be co-workers in your kingdom. In Jesus' name we pray. **Amen**.

29.

Lord God, this is our prayer, our hope, our commitment: that we might share in your work of redemption, bring hope to a hopeless world and share the light of Jesus with all whom we meet. We offer this money and dedicate it to your service. Receive our gifts and let them be used to bring the love of Christ to others. For it is in his name we ask it. **Amen**.

30.

Heavenly Father, these are our gifts, offered to you with grateful hearts. Take them and use them for your glory and for the extension of your kingdom. In the name of him who is our Lord and Saviour, Jesus Christ. **Amen**.

31.

In you, Lord God, is our salvation, our life, our future. You are everything to us and we love you. We bring our gifts, the money we have worked for and offer it to you with praise, with joy, with a sense of anticipation that you will enable us to use this money with wisdom and a proper sense of stewardship. Through Jesus Christ our Lord. **Amen**.

32.

Eternal God, you do not change, you are constant and faithful, always giving and always willing to welcome us into your presence. In your presence we give and dedicate this money and ourselves, willing and ready to use both as you desire. Accept these gifts in the name of Jesus. **Amen**.

Intercessions
and
Prayers on
specific themes

❧ ❧ ❧

INTERCESSIONS:

[handwritten: ✗ We pray especially for families of those killed in Afghanistan.]

[handwritten: Response]

1.

Living God, Bread of Life, we pray for the world and its needs.
Jesus our Lord, Bread of life: Hear us, help us, guide us

Living God, Bread of Life, we pray for the areas of the world torn apart by war or civil conflict. Sometimes the situations seem so huge and our contribution to solutions seems so small. Help us to respond in any way we can and not lose hope of finding peaceful and just solutions. We pray for those in positions of leadership, that they will find strength and courage for the task before them. We pray for those whose lives have been changed by war. Those who must fight. Those who have lost homes. Those who have lost a loved one. Those who have been injured in body, mind or spirit. Those who have lost any sense of hope that peace will come. Send your Spirit, Living God, that all people may work toward lasting peace.

Jesus our Lord, Bread of Life: Hear us, help us, guide us

Living God, Bread of Life, we pray for families and groups torn apart by conflict. Sometimes the situations are so difficult we prefer to pretend that they are unreal. Help us to hear the pain and conflict that individuals suffer in families and in other communities. We pray for those who hold positions of authority in such families and groups, those who misuse their power because of their own fear and need to control. We pray that they will find healthier ways to relate and exercise power. We pray for women who live in situations of violence, who are emotionally destroyed and have lost all sense of hope in a future without fear. We pray for children who are lost in a nightmare of abuse, without any means of escape. Send your Spirit, Living God, that we might hear the conflict and take appropriate action.

Jesus our Lord, Bread of Life: Hear us, help us, guide us

Living God, Bread of Life, we pray for Church communities torn apart by conflict. Sometimes we want to believe that your Body the Church is always a place of peace with people working and living in harmony together. Help us to work toward that ideal, by being honest and open about the conflicts that exist. We pray for ministers who feel lost and alone in situations of conflict. May they find healthy ways to deal with their own sense of loss as they lead others to face the conflict. We pray for those within the

22

Church who feel only the tension and pain of community life without any of the positive benefits. We pray for people who are disappointed by the anger and pain they find in Christian communities. We pray that you will give us strength and courage as we find ways to contribute to the health of our church life. Help us not to avoid the conflict because it is painful, but seek to work through the difficulties and emerge with a greater sense of wholeness. Send your Spirit, Living God, that we might bear with the tension and seek to create communities of growth.

Jesus our Lord, Bread of Life: **Hear us, help us, guide us**

active

Living God, Bread of Life, we are so disappointed by the conflict and tension within the human race. We want to be good people living in peace, and yet so often we do not or cannot. We are all so different and have so many different needs. You created us in our variety and uniqueness and have given us the skills we need to create communities of wholeness. Send your Spirit, Living God, that we might constantly seek your ways of living whole in our various communities.

Jesus our Lord, Bread of Life: **Hear us, help us, guide us**

We offer our prayers in Jesus' name and in the power of the Holy Spirit. **Amen**.

2.

Father God, so often the needs of others seem so vast and we so small, and yet you call us to intercede:

We hold out to you, Almighty God
the violence
the hatred
the anger
the abuse
and the self-centredness of this world.

We remember that Jesus came to show us the way of
peace
love
forgiveness
justice
and self-giving.

Open our eyes and ears
hearts and minds
that we might work where we are:

to give up our violence . . . . . for your peace
to give up our hatred . . . . . . for your love
to give up our anger . . . . for your forgiveness
to give up our abuse . . . . for your justice
to give up our self-centredness for your self-giving.

Almighty God, change your world and begin with us,
in Jesus' name we pray. **Amen**.

3.

We pray for the needs of others, knowing you delight to hear
our prayers.

We pray for your Church throughout the world, that men and
women of faith will follow you and stand firm for truth and
justice.

Lord hear us: and graciously renew us

We pray for world leaders and any who exercise authority, that
power would not corrupt, that those responsible for the lives of
others would work honestly and with integrity for the good of all.

Lord hear us: and graciously renew us

We pray for men and women courageous enough to work for
peace and justice, that they may know your presence as guide
and comforter.

Lord hear us: and graciously renew us

We pray for those who suffer in body, mind or spirit, the sick and
dying, those alone, those afraid, those who mourn, those who
have lost faith in the goodness of life, that your light and love
might shine in their darkness and bring the possibility of
comfort, encouragement and peace.

Lord hear us: and graciously renew us

We pray for ourselves, that we might seek your will for us and follow you with determination and trust.

Lord hear us: and graciously renew us

Fill us afresh with your Holy Spirit, that forgiven and renewed we may face our daily life, filled with your love and working with you in this world.

Lord hear us: and graciously renew us

Through Jesus Christ, our Lord and Redeemer. **Amen.**

4.

Let us bring our prayers to the Heavenly Father,
knowing he loves us and longs to hear us.

Let us pray for the Body of Christ, the Church of God throughout the world. May all Christian communities be centres of healing and hope in a broken world. We pray for this church and all who worship here. For all who serve in this church: minister, stewards, pastoral visitors, workers with children and young people, treasurer and stewards of property: may they know your guidance as they respond to your call, seeking to serve you and this community. Renew them for their work. Refresh us all and enable us to shine with the light of Jesus.

Light of the world: Shine in us

Let us pray for the nations of the world, for governments and leaders. May all who hold positions of authority be moved to seek justice and peace and serve those they lead with integrity and care. We pray for our own country and government, that party politics and individual ambition would never be an excuse for failing to serve the good of society. We pray that Christians will be involved in local and national government, bringing the light of Jesus into the political arena.

Light of the world: Shine in us

Let us pray for countries and communities damaged or destroyed by war. May all who are in positions of leadership be courageous enough to seek peaceful and just solutions. We remember all who suffer as a result of war. Those made homeless, those injured in body or mind, and those who grieve the loss of a loved one. We pray that they will find support from family, friends and society as they come to terms with their experiences. We pray for all agencies working to help those in the midst of war. May they be strengthened and renewed as they bring practical help, comfort and hope.

Light of the world: Shine in us

Let us pray for those who are sick, especially those known to us. We remember those who care for a sick loved one. We pray for those whose days are filled with pain. May they know your healing love and be filled with a sense of hope. We pray for all who work in the healing professions. May they be sensitive to the needs of those they serve.

Light of the world: Shine in us

Almighty God, you long to hear our prayers and concerns. We bring these our prayers to you, trusting in your grace. Fill us afresh to serve you in the world, that we might reflect the light of Jesus.

Light of the world: Shine in us

Through Jesus Christ, our Lord and Saviour. **Amen**.

5.

Let us bring our petitions before the Father, asking his blessing on the many situations of concern to us.
Let us come with confidence to the Father, in the Spirit's energy and with the strong name of Jesus to support and guide us as we pray.

Lord, hear our petition: and draw us closer to yourself

Father God, we pray for the Church throughout the world,
for the worldwide body of people seeking to love and
    know you better
and follow you more closely;
for the churches in this area
for the church in this place.
Empower all church communities to be what you
    would have them be.

Lord, hear our petition: and draw us closer to yourself

Father God, we pray for the world,
areas torn apart by war and conflict
places of hunger and thirst.
Empower us to meet the needs of so many.

Lord, hear our petition: and draw us closer to yourself

Father God, we pray for our country
for people in positions of authority,
for leaders and led.
Empower the people of this country to live and work for the good
of all.

Lord, hear our petition: and draw us closer to yourself

Father God, we pray for those who are sick and lonely
for those who mourn
for those struggling with illness
for those who have lost faith in you and in life.
Empower them, that they may find healing, hope and
encouragement.

Lord, hear our petition: and draw us closer to yourself

Father God, we pray for ourselves.
Empower us to be a people of vision and hope.
Move us by your Holy Spirit to be your people in this place.

Lord hear our petition: and draw us closer to yourself

In the dynamic name of Jesus we bring our prayers; empower us
to listen for the answers. **Amen.**

6.
Let us bring our prayers to God.

Everlasting God, we pray for the many needs of your world, the
needs we know about personally, the needs we hear about
through friends and the media.

God of goodness and grace, hear our prayer

Let us pray to the Father for the Church.
For the Church throughout the world, a body of people held
together by the bonds of Jesus' love.

For the Church in this area, a body of people connected
    to a greater whole.
For our own church, a body of people linked by the Holy Spirit
    to a wider Church and vision.
For hurting people within church communities.
For all who preach and teach your word.
For all who offer themselves freely day by day to your service.
For all who feel excluded or rejected.

(silence)

Father, sanctify your Church, consecrate our lives and
    anoint us for service.

God of goodness and grace, hear our prayer

Let us pray to the Father for the world.
For people throughout the world linked by a common bond
    of humanity.
For countries throughout the world locked in war or conflict.
For people who hunger and thirst for daily food and water.
For people who have little or no access to the medical care
    we take for granted.
For people who suffer physically, emotionally or spiritually
    at the hands of others.
For the homeless and the refugee.

(silence)

Father, sanctify your world, and anoint us with the courage to
challenge prejudice, inequity, intolerance and hatred.

God of goodness and grace, hear our prayer

Let us pray to the Father for our own community,
the people we know who are in need of our support.
Those who are sick
Those who are struggling with faith
Those who are mourning
For our minister and family
For our stewards, Sunday School teachers and Class Leaders
For our steward of property and finance
For our flower arrangers and cleaners
For those who are no longer able to come to church because of
    old age or infirmity
For each other.

(silence)

Father, sanctify us, and anoint us with the grace we need to live together a supportive, nurturing, caring community.

God of goodness and grace, hear our prayer

Everlasting God, we bring our prayers for the many needs of your world. Hear us we pray, for we pray in the name of our Lord and Saviour, Jesus Christ. **Amen**.

* * * *

SPECIFIC THEMES:

7.
FOR GOD'S PEOPLE

Eternal God, we are your people; in your Son you have redeemed us; by your Spirit you have sealed us as your own.

We are old and young, big and small,
    new to faith and long in faith.
We are a strange mixture of people
    held together by our love for you
and desire to worship and serve you.

We have many needs, sometimes the same needs, sometimes different needs. Sometimes we are strong and able to support others, sometimes we are weak and vulnerable and in need of support. We are a strange mixture of people held together by your grace.

We have many ideas about how to worship you.
Some of us need silence, time for meditation and reflection.
Some of us need exuberant noise, space to clap
    and dance our praises.
Some of us need lots of different ways to worship.
We are a strange mixture of people
    held together by your Spirit's strength.

We have many ideas about how to serve you and
    respond to your call.
Some of us are upfront people, out there and visible.
Some of us are quiet, behind the scenes people.
Some of us are in between. We are preachers, cleaners, flower
arrangers, stewards, money people, property people, musicians
and singers.
We are a strange mixture of people, held together by your love.

Eternal God, we are your people, the same, yet different, and we
know you rejoice in those differences, for you created each one of
us to be unique.

Come to us now, eternal God, and meet our varied needs, enable
us to be the strange mixture that we are and enable us to rejoice
in our common calling to serve and worship you.

Through Jesus Christ our Lord. **Amen**.

8.
STILLNESS

Lord, there is so much activity in our lives
We rush and hurry, always wanting to be somewhere else
hardly time to stop and think
hardly time to be with you.
Lord, why do we spend so much time on the run?
Help us to find a balance
of activity and stillness,
Some time to listen to your voice within:
Be still and know that I am God.
We would be still and know

Lord, there is so much activity in our lives
So many things and people to claim our attention
So many good things for us to spend our time on,
and yet there is hardly time
to pause for any one thing.
How do we choose which is important?
How can we know when enough is enough?
Lord, why do we spend so much time on the run?

Help us to find a balance
of activity and stillness,
Some time to listen to your voice within:
Be still and know that I am God.

We would be still and know

Lord, there is so much activity in our lives
So many meetings and places and people,
filling our days with their demands and their noise.
Lord, why do we spend so much time on the run?
Help us to find a balance
of activity and stillness,
Some time to listen to your voice within:
Be still and know that I am God.

We would be still and know

Lord, there is so much activity in our lives
Yet when we look at your life,
at the example you set for us,
we see clearly your greatest work,
the work of salvation,
took place when you were physically restrained,
unable to move, inactive, still.
Lord, help us to yield our business to you,
to rest in your grace and listen for
that still, small voice.

In Jesus' name we ask it and for his sake.   **Amen**.

9.
TEMPTATION

Confession:

Lord God, we confess our failure to withstand temptation.
Before we know it the unkind words and
thoughtless actions are said and done,
hurting another, causing pain and creating barriers.

Our lives are littered with the sad words 'if only'.
If only they hadn't provoked us
If only they had been different
If only we hadn't said those things
If only we hadn't thought those things
If only we hadn't done those things
If only

(*silence*)

Lord God, forgive us; help us not to be overwhelmed
    by our failures.

You know how often we fail to meet temptation head on and
emerge victorious. Forgive us for the times of failure. Help us to
keep on trying and to look forward with hope, saying: 'next time'.
Next time by the grace of Jesus we will be victorious.

In the strong name of Jesus we claim forgiveness and
    a new beginning. **Amen**.

Praise and Thanksgiving:

Father God,
we praise and adore you
You are creator of all things
and worthy of our love and praise.

We thank you that you have shown us the example of your Son,
who faced temptation and emerged victorious.

Jesus, you share our humanity
You knew temptation
and trusted in the strength of God the Father.

Thank you, Lord Jesus, for facing temptation in the desert.
Tempted to forsake God
Tempted to worship evil
Tempted to perform miracles to meet your own needs,
You withstood all temptations for our sakes.
Thank you, Lord.

When our faith is tempted, you are able to lead us out of temptation.
Thank you, Lord.
Amen.

10.
HEALING AND WHOLENESS

Intercessions:

God of salvation, healing and wholeness, we bring our prayers to you that we might know your salvation, healing and wholeness.

We pray for people who are ill, in hospital or at home.

(*silence*)

We pray for people who are ill, physically, mentally,
         emotionally or spiritually.

(*silence*)

We pray for people who are struggling to come to terms with limitations, physical, mental, emotional or spiritual.

(*silence*)

Lord God, may each one be filled with strength, find the will to fight against despair and be able to put their trust in your presence and grace.

We pray for people who are caring for a sick loved one.

(*silence*)

We pray for people who are caring for a disabled relative or friend.

(*silence*)

We pray for children who are caring for a sick or disabled parent.

(*silence*)

Lord God, may each one know the value of what they do, find space for themselves and accept help that is offered by other people.

We pray for people who are dying and those who watch with them.

(silence)

We pray for people who are mourning the loss of a loved one.

(silence)

We pray for people who are contemplating suicide

(silence)

Lord God, may each one find a way to share their feelings and fears and discover new opportunities for wholeness.

We pray for people who are afraid of pain and loneliness.

(silence)

We pray for people who feel lost and confused.

(silence)

We pray for people who have lost faith in you.

(silence)

Lord God, may each one be filled with courage, find joy in life and have a sense of hope for the future.

We pray for people who offer medical help and emotional or spiritual support and care.

(silence)

We pray for doctors
for nurses
for psychiatrists
for counsellors
for ministers

(silence)

Lord God, may each one work with sensitivity and care, seek the best for those they help and know where they can find support when needed.

God of salvation, healing and wholeness, we bring our prayers to you, in the name of Jesus Christ our Lord, who came that we might know your salvation, healing and wholeness. **Amen**.

11.
SEXUAL ABUSE

Intercessions:

In the name of Jesus and through the power of the Holy Spirit, we bring our prayers to God our Father.

Living God, we know that there is misunderstanding and ignorance concerning the sexual abuse of children. Such abuse continues because of secrecy, fear and shame. Give us the willingness to listen to those who have survived the trauma, and enable us to become better informed, that our churches may become places of hope and healing.

Lord of wholeness; pour out your Spirit on each one of us

Living God, we know that there are men, women and children who live today with the ongoing effects of childhood abuse. People who find it hard to trust others, or believe in themselves. People who find it hard to make and sustain relationships. People whose lives are less than you intended them to be. Give us the willingness to listen to their stories and validate their feelings. Give us the courage to walk with them along the path of healing and wholeness. And give them all they need to seek the fullness of life which Jesus died to bring.

Lord of wholeness; pour out your Spirit on each one of us

Living God, we know that there are people who still cannot tell another person of the abuse they suffered in childhood. People who are afraid of what others will think. People who remain afraid of their abuser. People who have no sense of hope that the future could be different. Give us the willingness to be open to the possibility of their abuse. Give us the courage to give of ourselves by offering comfort and belief. And give to all who are afraid to tell, a sense that there is hope.

Lord of wholeness; pour out your Spirit on each one of us

Living God, we know there are children being abused now, as we pray, by a parent, by a step-parent, by a sibling, by a trusted adult friend, by a figure in authority. Give us the willingness to enter into their pain. Give us the ability to walk in their shoes. Give the courage to fight for their right to a childhood free of abuse. Give them the courage to say 'no' and to seek out those who can help.

Lord of wholeness; pour out your Spirit on each one of us

Living God, we know that right now children are calling Childline or the Samaritans, a step that takes tremendous courage. May they be met with kindness and sensitivity, and together find a way to stop the abuse. May those who will receive such calls be open and honest, and offer encouragement and support.

Lord of wholeness; pour out your Spirit on each one of us

Living God, we know your word tells us that Jesus is the light of the world. He comes to dispel the darkness. In his name we pray that the darkness surrounding the abuse of our children will be illuminated. We pray that the chains of fear, pain and secrecy will be broken and that the light of Christ will shine in the lives of those who are survivors, bringing healing and wholeness.

Lord of wholeness; pour out your Spirit on each one of us

In the name of Jesus, the light of the world we bring our prayers. **Amen**.

12.
THE LORD'S PRAYER
Our Father, who art in heaven
(*silence*)

Lord God, you have asked us to call you our Father, for you are the Father of us all. We come as your children, knowing you long to hear us, and long to reveal more of yourself to us.

We pray for those for whom the word Father has been corrupted and spoilt by their experiences of imperfect earthly fathers. May they come to know your fatherhood as something good, something safe and secure. Enable us to grow in understanding of your fatherhood and never let us take our relationship with you for granted.

(silence)

Hallowed be thy name
(silence)

Lord God, we hallow your name; we call you holy, for that is what you are. We pray that every time we use your name it will be with an awareness of whom we are speaking about. May all people learn of your holiness and may we never take your name in vain.

(silence)

Thy kingdom come;
thy will be done;
on earth as it is in heaven
(silence)

Lord God, we pray so glibly for your will to be done, for your kingdom to come. Help us to grasp what it means for your will to be done in each of our lives. Give us strength and courage as we commit ourselves to seeking and doing your will. May all Christians let your kingdom come in them.

(silence)

Give us this day our daily bread
(silence)

Lord God, we pray for all that we need to live well each day, food for body, mind and spirit. Help us to use wisely of the abundance we have. We pray for those for whom daily bread is a luxury. We remember their needs. And we ask for the vision and motivation to change a world where some die of hunger whilst others have much more than they could ever use.

(silence)

And forgive us our trespasses, as
we forgive those who trespass
against us
(silence)

Lord God, we confess our sins to you; the sins of omission and commission. Forgive us, we pray, and restore us into a right relationship with you.

We pray for those who find forgiving others an impossible task. Be patient with them, Lord, and help us to be understanding.

We ask that they will continue to seek your forgiveness, and that they will come to the place of healing and release, finding courage to forgive those who have hurt them. Lord, teach us how to forgive each other that we may live in harmony and be restored into right relationships with each other.

(*silence*)

And lead us not into temptation;
but deliver us from evil
(*silence*)

Lord God, we are so easily led, so easily tempted. Keep us close to you so that when temptation comes we might be able to resist it in the strength that Christ gives. We pray for those who have given in to temptation and feel lost and devastated. May they find your loving presence, and forgiveness, and be able to move on from this time of trial.

We pray for each other that we might not be misled by the apparent good in life, but seek always to do your will in your way.

(*silence*)

For thine is the kingdom, the power
and the glory, for ever and ever.
Amen.

13.
CREED

We believe in you, Father
Creator of all that is.
We believe in you, Jesus
hands tied, vulnerable
at the disposal of others.
We believe in your ability
to understand suffering.
We see you, stripped, beaten
absorbing anger and hatred.
Rejected but not overwhelmed.

We believe in the Holy Spirit
the giver of life.
Light, guide, comforter, enabler.
We believe in God
Father, Son and Spirit
Community.
Amen.

The Christian year
and other
special days

ADVENT

Advent Confession:
Living Word, Word of God,
Word made flesh.
Come to us again with your word of forgiveness.

We confess the sinfulness of so many of our words.

Forgive the hasty words that destroy

(*silence*)

the thoughtless words that cause pain

(*silence*)

the unkind words that divide

(*silence*)

Forgive the words we use that divide your people and separate us
    from one another.
Let our words be your words,

Words of love that heal

(*silence*)

Words of encouragement that build up

(*silence*)

Words of hope that bring life

(*silence*)

Word of God, Living Word
Word made flesh
Come to us again with your word of forgiveness, that we might be
    your word in the world.

Through Jesus Christ our Lord.
Amen.

Advent/Christmas Thanksgiving:

Lord God, we come with our thanks for all your goodness to us.

God the Father, we give you thanks and praise,
for you are our creator, you call us and equip us and
    send us out.

God the Son, Jesus our Lord, we give you thanks and praise,
for you are our Redeemer, you gave yourself that we might be
free, and you bring us your peace which is beyond
understanding.

God the Holy Spirit, we give you thanks and praise,
for you are our comforter, you challenge us and prod us when we
are complacent, you enable us to be who we are in Jesus and
draw us closer to the Father.

Father, Son and Holy Spirit, we give you thanks and praise,
for you have carried us in our weakness, sustained us in our
need and equipped us to follow.

Accept our thanks and praise, offered in the name of Jesus to
your glory.
Amen.

ADVENT 1

Collect:

Eternal God, you have set hope in the hearts of your people, and we are amazed by your activity in our world. Keep us hoping for change and renewal, that all people may come to know your love, through Jesus Christ our Lord. **Amen**.

Praise:

Eternal God, we your people gather to worship.
For your raising up prophets and leaders to proclaim and live your word:

We praise you

For your continued presence in our lives and
loving concern for us:

We praise you

For your call to follow:

We praise you

Jesus, our Lord, we your people gather to worship.
For coming among us as a child, one of us:

We praise you

For your ministry of healing, salvation and wholeness:

We praise you

For bringing to us fullness of life;

We praise you

God the Holy Spirit, we your people gather to worship.
For your enabling presence throughout the generations:

We praise you

For your constant encouragement and challenge:

We praise you

For drawing us always closer to Christ:

We praise you

Eternal God, Father, Son and Holy Spirit, we your people gather
to worship.
Accept our praise, offered in the name of Jesus and through your
Holy Spirit. **Amen**.

Confession:

Living God,
Forgive the words, thoughts and actions which are hasty and
painful to others.
Forgive the unwillingness to hear and obey your call.
Forgive the indifference that stops us from seeing how we have
hurt you and each other.
Forgive the apathy that prevents us doing from your will.

Cleanse us, we pray, and recreate us in your image. Restore our
confidence and hope in you that we might walk in your way of
love, through your Son, Jesus Christ our Redeemer. **Amen**.

Intercessions:

Brothers and Sisters in Christ, the Lord of Hope longs to hear our
prayers. Let us come with confidence and hope to our heavenly
Father, seeking his way and his will.

Eternal God, renew our hope
Give us confidence to believe in change

Eternal God, as we look at the world in which we live we are often
filled with despair. In our newspapers and on our televisions we
see the evidence of our inability to live in peace. It would be so
easy for us to believe that you are absent from the world; it would
be easy to give up our hopes and dreams for equality, justice and
peace for all people.

Eternal God, renew our hope
Give us confidence to believe in change

Eternal God, as we see and hear about wars; as we observe
greed, selfishness and self-centredness; as we hear about
oppression, injustice, pain and suffering in many forms, it would
be easy for us to believe that the world is beyond redemption.
Yet you sent your Son to redeem the world and you call us to
continue his work of redemption. It would be so easy for us to

give up our hopes and dreams of a world renewed by your Holy Spirit.

Eternal God, renew our hope
Give us confidence to believe in change

Eternal God, as we recognise our own destructive actions and words; as we acknowledge our inability to be forgiving and loving; as we accept our own contribution to the sins of the world, it would be easy for us to believe that we are fools. It would be so easy for us to give up our hopes and dreams of a Church united in your love and modelling a new way of being community.

Eternal God, renew our hope
Give us confidence to believe in change

Eternal God, we recognise our humanness, our imperfections, and yet we cling with confidence to your love for us. Our hope is not in the best efforts of people but in your eternal patience and grace. In the power of your Spirit we have hopes and dreams for a Church, for a society, for a world, where people are valued and esteemed, where strength and power are used wisely, where need and vulnerability are met with support, and where all people work together to serve the common good.

Eternal God, renew our hope
Give us confidence to believe in change

Eternal God, we offer our prayers in confidence, in the name of Jesus and in the power of your Spirit.
Amen.

ADVENT 2

Collect:

Almighty God, we celebrate your coming in Jesus, the Word made flesh. As we worship, come to us anew that we might be filled with your love. Through Jesus Christ our Lord. **Amen.**

Praise:

Living God, you have given us your word to live by
  and we praise you.

Loving God, you have given us your word of life in Jesus Christ
  and we praise you.

Giving God, you have brought us your word of comfort,
  challenge and encouragement in your Holy Spirit
  and we praise you.

Eternal God, you have given us your active word;
  bringing order out of chaos
  light out of darkness
  hope out of despair
  life out of death
  and we praise you.

Living, loving, giving God, your word is life to us
  and we praise you.
Through Jesus Christ our Lord. **Amen.**

Thanksgiving:

Living God, we thank you for your word by which we find life.

We thank you for those who have faithfully proclaimed your word, beginning with the prophets and leaders of your people Israel, and through all the generations since.

Living God, we thank you for your word by which we find life

We thank you for those who have faithfully recorded your word. For the men and women who have translated your word. For those whose painstaking task it is to enable your word to be read by many peoples. For those who take risks to bring your written

45

word to people seeking to follow you in situations of oppression and fear.

Living God, we thank you for your word by which we find life

We thank you for those who shared your word with us. For those who enabled us to see and hear your word of life. For their faithfulness in living your word.

Living God, we thank you for your word by which we find life

Enable us by your Spirit to be bearers of your word in the world. Through Jesus Christ our Lord. **Amen**.

Confession:

Living Word, Word of God,
Word made flesh.
Come to us again with your word of forgiveness.

We confess the sinfulness of so many of our words.

Forgive the hasty words that destroy

(*silence*)

the thoughtless words that cause pain

(*silence*)

the unkind words that divide

(*silence*)

Forgive the words we use that divide your people and
    separate us from one another.
Let our words be your words,

Words of love that heal

(*silence*)

Words of encouragement that build up

(*silence*)

Words of hope that bring life

(*silence*)

Word of God, Living Word,
Word made flesh,
Come to us again with your word of forgiveness,
that we might be your word in the world.
Through Jesus Christ our Lord. **Amen**.

Intercessions:

Father God, we know that words are powerful tools that can be used for good or ill. Words can build up or destroy. Living Word, Word of Life, we bring our concerns, our needs and the needs of others. Help us to pray with clean hearts and listen for your word to us.

Living Word, Word of Life; renew us

God our Father, we pray for people whose words build up, encourage and challenge us.
For those who preach and teach the gospel.
For those who heal the sick and comfort the suffering.
For those who care in so many places and situations of pain
    and difficulty.
For those who support people in living well with illness
    or disability.
For those who teach in our schools, colleges and universities,
    and Sunday Schools.
For those who use words to share poetry and literature.
For those who call us to involvement in the life of society.
For those who help us to see how we can change the world.

(*silence*)

Living Word, Word of Life; renew us

God our Father, we pray for those whose words are bitter,
    angry and destructive.
For those who have lost faith in you and in life.
For those who have been hurt by another person.
For those who have lost hope in life.
For those who are unjust.
For those who hate.
For those who contemplate self-destruction.

(*silence*)

Living Word, Word of Life; renew us

God our Father, we pray for those whose words have led to
   reconciliation, peace, forgiveness and hope.
For those who comfort the prisoner.
For those who have said they are sorry.
For those who work against injustice.

(*silence*)

Living Word, Word of Life; renew us

God our Father, we pray for those whose words have led to
   hatred, divisions and war.
For those who oppress other people.
For those who support unjust regimes.
For those who use torture as a means of control.
For those who believe violence is the answer to a problem.

(*silence*)

Living Word, Word of Life; renew us

God our Father, accept our prayers in the name of Jesus,
   the living Word.   **Amen**.

ADVENT 3

Collect:

Lord God, you sent John the Baptist to prepare the people for your coming. Help us to prepare for your coming with the same sense of urgency, that when you finally come in glory we will be prepared, ready to take our place in your kingdom. Through Jesus Christ our Lord. **Amen**.

Praise and Thanksgiving:

Lord God, we give you thanks and praise
You sent John the Baptist to prepare the way
You gave him a message of repentance
You sent your prophets to announce his coming
You have sent people throughout the ages to proclaim our need for readiness and repentance.
We give you thanks and praise

Lord God, we give you thanks and praise
You sent John the Baptist to prepare the people for the coming
    of Jesus
You sent him to call the people to repentance and baptism
You have sent people throughout the ages to preach and baptise
    in your name.
We give you thanks and praise

Lord God, you call us to prepare for your coming. As we celebrate your coming in the Christ-child we also prepare for Christ to come again. You have not left us alone, but given us your Holy Spirit, and promised that your Son will come back.
We give you thanks and praise

Lord God, prepare our hearts to receive you this Christmas and when you come in glory.
Through Jesus Christ our Lord, who comes to us again and again. **Amen**.

Confession:

Lord God, creator, sustainer
and source of all life,
Coming in the Christ-child, dwelling in us.
We confess our inability to serve you wholeheartedly.
Forgive us the times we diminish another.
Forgive us the times we rob another of their true value
    and worth.
Forgive us the times we hurt and destroy the people closest to us.
Forgive us the times we forget your way of love and peace.

Creator God, coming in the Christ-child
Come again to us
Forgive us
Restore us
Fill us again with a fresh determination to follow you.

Through Jesus Christ our Lord. **Amen.**

Intercessions:

Lord, hear our prayers, for we have many concerns,
    worries and needs.

(*silence*)

We bring them to you, the prayers we can speak and the prayers
of our hearts that cannot be put into words.
Lord, you keep coming to us;   *LORD IN YOUR MERCY*
come afresh with your Spirit's power   *HEAR OUR PRAYER*

Lord, hear our prayers for the world,
    our many concerns and worries.

(*silence*)

You called John the Baptist to a prophetic ministry, challenging
the people's behaviours and attitudes. May we find our prophetic
voice, and challenge people's behaviours and attitudes.
Lord, you keep coming to us;   *Help us to also use a prophetic voice*
come afresh with your Spirit's power

Lord, hear our prayers for your Church,
    our many concerns and worries.

(*silence*)

You called John the Baptist to a prophetic ministry, challenging the apathy and sinfulness of the religious people. May we hear your prophetic voice challenging us and calling us to repentance.

Lord, you keep coming to us;
come afresh with your Spirit's power

Lord, hear our prayers for the world,
    our many concerns and worries.

(*silence*)

You have called us to be leaven for the world yet so often we simply fit in with the prevailing philosophy. May we find a voice to challenge the arrogant, to speak for the powerless and proclaim your healing love in a world that seems bent on destruction.

Lord, you keep coming to us;
come afresh with your Spirit's power

Lord, hear our prayers for your people,
    our many concerns and worries.

(*silence*)

You have called us to serve, to go into all the world and make disciples. We are slow and hesitant witnesses of you, foolish and afraid. May we find a voice to shape the world, to share good news and bring all people into love and knowledge of you.

Lord, you keep coming to us;
come afresh with your Spirit's power

Lord, hear our prayers, our many concerns and worries

(*silence*)

We remember all who are ill, in body, mind or spirit
We remember all who are grieving
We remember all who are lost and alone, afraid of life
We remember all who are struggling to make sense of the world
    and their faith
May we find a voice to comfort the sad, aid the stranger and
    share ourselves with others in need.

Lord, you keep coming to us;
come afresh with your Spirit's power

Lord, hear our prayers, our many concerns and worries. We bring them in the name of Jesus, our strength and Redeemer.
Amen.

ADVENT 4

Collect:

Almighty God, as Mary found the courage to say 'Yes' to your plan for her life, so may we be courageous enough to go where you send and believe in your impossible call. Through Jesus Christ our Lord. **Amen**.

Praise:

Impossible God, your creativity astounds us
    your plans amaze us
    your power confounds us
Impossible God, we worship and adore you.

Impossible God, your redemption saves us from selfishness
    your love overwhelms us
    your grace welcomes us
Impossible God, we worship and adore you.

Impossible God, your commands challenge us
    your Spirit enfolds us
    your call follows us
Impossible God, we worship and adore you.

Impossible God, you are worthy of our worship and praise, which we offer in the name of him who fulfilled your impossible plan of salvation, our Lord Jesus Christ. **Amen**.

Confession:

God, with whom nothing is impossible
forgive the blindness that stops us seeing
forgive the noise that stops us hearing
forgive the self that blocks out the possibility of the impossible.
God, with whom nothing is impossible, forgive us and cleanse us
send your Holy Spirit to renew us
and restore us into a right relationship
with you and each other.
Through Jesus Christ our Lord. **Amen**.

Intercessions:

Almighty God, you need our 'yes' of obedience to your call. Imperfect though we are, and living in a fallen world as we do, you call us to be involved in every area of our society. There are many seemingly impossible situations in which we fulfil our call to be your people.

We remember people who have said 'yes' to serving others:
our royal family
our MPs and government, local and national
those who uphold our laws, the police, the courts
our firefighters
those who serve in the forces
We pray for them and for their continued work.

(*silence*)

Lord, hear our prayer

We remember people who have said 'yes' to serving others:
our doctors and nurses
our social workers and counsellors
missionaries at home and abroad
our ambulance workers and paramedics
our ministers
We pray for them and for their continued work.

(*silence*)

Lord, hear our prayer

We remember people who have said 'yes' to serving others:
our teachers
those who entertain us
those whose words of poetry bring pleasure
those whose music lifts our spirits
We pray for them and for their continued work.

(*silence*)

Lord, hear our prayer

We remember seemingly impossible situations:
children abused by another family member or an authority figure
women beaten by a partner
individuals with no job and little hope of finding one
people who feel lonely or abandoned by family and society
We pray for them, seeking change in their situations.

53

(*silence*)

Lord, hear our prayer

We remember seemingly impossible situations:
countries at war, race against race
individuals tortured for their faith in you
people imprisoned for their political beliefs
We pray for them, seeking change in their situations.

(*silence*)

Lord, hear our prayer

We remember seemingly impossible situations:
people in countries where there is not enough food
    or clean drinking water
countries where disease and lack of food shorten the
    expected life span
countries struggling against natural disaster,
    earthquakes and floods
We pray for them, seeking change in their situations.

(*silence*)

Lord, hear our prayer

Almighty God, we know that with you nothing is impossible. Help us to say 'yes' to your call to be involved in the world, bringing your love to bear in the many impossible situations we face. In Jesus' name we bring our prayers, trusting in his presence with us as we go into the world. **Amen**.

CHRISTMAS DAY

Collect:

Lord God, we celebrate your coming in the Christ-child,
we reflect on your giving and loving.
As we worship you,
fill us with the courage to be obedient to your will as he was
    obedient to your will,
to your eternal glory.
Through Jesus Christ our Lord.
Amen.

Praise and Thanksgiving:

You, Lord, are worthy of our praise and thanksgiving.
Today we give you thanks for the gift of your Son, Jesus,
who comes to dispel our darkness.

Living God, light of the world, we praise and thank you:
A Son is given, a child is born for us.
Lord God, we celebrate your coming with our thanks and praise.
Lord God, we celebrate your giving with our thanks and praise.
Lord God, we celebrate your loving with our thanks and praise.

Living God, light of the world, we praise and thank you:
We celebrate the birth of your Son.
We celebrate his life.
We celebrate his giving of himself in death and
    resurrection for us.

You, Lord, are worthy of our thanks and praise, today and
always, through Jesus Christ our Lord, our Light, our Salvation.
Amen.

Confession:

Lord God, as we celebrate your coming, we confess that we have
failed to shine with the light of Jesus.
We get caught up in our own plans and wants, and somehow you
get pushed aside.
Forgive us, Lord

We concentrate on the wrong things, and somehow forget the
reason for our celebrations.

Forgive us, Lord

We become selfish and inward looking and somehow we lose
sight of your vision for us.

Forgive us, Lord

Lord God, accept our prayers,
forgive our sins, and renew us for our continued walk with you.
Through Jesus Christ our Lord.   **Amen.**

Intercessions:

Lord God, as we celebrate your coming we are aware of the needs
of many people and bring our prayers for them to you.
Lord God, we pray for people for whom Christmas is a time to
celebrate your coming:

    for your Church, the body of your Son
    for all ministers and preachers
    for all who will worship you today
    for all who are away from their loved ones because they
        are serving you
    for all who are providing food or support for others this day.
Lord God, let all Christians celebrate with joy the coming of
    your Son.

Let the light of Christ shine in us and through us

Lord God, we pray for people for whom Christmas is simply a
reminder of what they do not have:

    for those who live alone and have no one to share
        this special day with,
    for children who have run away from home and will spend
        Christmas on the streets,
    for people who have lost a loved one and are painfully
        reminded of that loss at this time of year,
    for people who feel they are failing their families because
        they cannot keep up with the material and commercial
        aspects of this season.
Lord God, may all people find hope for the future and discover
the support of others in their time of need.

Let the light of Christ shine in us and through us

Lord God, we pray for people for whom Christmas will be spent in difficult situations:

> for people who are in the midst of war
> for people who are in hospital
> for people who are in abusive families
> for people who are homeless
> for people who are hungry
> for people who are lonely and afraid.

Lord God, give us true gratitude for all that we have and an awareness that this is a painful and difficult time for many people.

Let the light of Christ shine in us and through us

Lord God, we bring our prayers in the name of the one whose birth we celebrate, our Lord Jesus Christ. **Amen**.

EPIPHANY

Intercessions:

As the wise men came so long ago, so we come seeking Jesus for the Church, for the world, for ourselves.

We come seeking Jesus for the Church.
Lord, we pray for ·the Church, its leaders, its members, its witness and service.

(*silence*)

Lord, we offer you the frankincense of worship. May your Church be renewed and recreated in your image, may we be challenged to growth and maturity, may we offer all that we are to your service.

We come seeking Jesus for our worship and our life together.
Lord Jesus come, guide us and keep us.

We come seeking Jesus for the world.
Lord, we pray for the world, its resources, its people, its life and future.

(*silence*)

Lord, we offer you the gold of wealth. May your world be renewed and recreated, may we be challenged to use our wealth wisely, may we learn not to misuse and abuse the abundant resources of the world.

We come seeking Jesus for our wealth and our life together.
Lord Jesus come, guide us and keep us.

We come seeking Jesus for ourselves.
Lord, we pray for ourselves, our families and friends,
situations, people and places that concern us.

(*silence*)

Lord, we offer you the myrrh of our suffering and pain. We remember people sick and lonely. People bereaved and fearful. People oppressed and powerless. People suffering in any way, physically or mentally or spiritually. May all these people be renewed and recreated, finding comfort, strength and support in you, in family and in friends.

58

We come seeking Jesus for the myrrh of our suffering and pain. Lord Jesus come, guide us and keep us.

Lord Jesus, hear our prayers, for the Church, the world, for ourselves, for it is in your name we come.
Amen.

ASH WEDNESDAY

Collect:

Here we are, Lord God, in faith and penitence, knowing you to be loving and forgiving. Be present with us in this time of worship, that we might know a fresh touch of your Holy Spirit; and know ourselves to be forgiven and renewed. Through Jesus Christ our Lord. **Amen**.

Confession:

On this day we draw close to you, eternal God
aware of your patient love
and our own sinfulness.
We confess our sins, humbly trusting in your mercy.

(*silence*)

Forgive us, we pray, for so often we fall short of your call to follow. We are hesitant disciples, fearful of the consequences of standing firm in our faith.

Forgive us, we pray, for so often we fall short of your call to service. We are foolish disciples, fearful of being hurt or misunderstood, so sure we know better than you the way we should go.

We are sorry for the times we let you and ourselves down. Forgive us we pray, in the name of our Lord Jesus, and send your Holy Spirit, that we might be renewed, ready to follow and serve you in the world. **Amen**.

Praise and Thanksgiving:

Almighty and Eternal God
Your patient love has pursued us
Your steadfast love has held us
Your gracious love has guided us.

Your majesty and power are beyond our imagination.
By your word worlds are created.
At your command the Son comes, bringing salvation and hope.
You are a Holy God, rich in love and abundant in blessings for your people.
We praise and adore you.

On this day we come with thankful hearts
for you are steadfast.
You reach out and embrace us
Your Son comes, offering himself

And we thank you.

Father, Son and Holy Spirit, we give you thanks and praise.
Amen.

Intercessions:

On this day we draw close to you, bringing our concerns for a sinful and needy world.

We pray for your Church. Forgive the sins committed in your name because of our arrogance and prejudice. May all Christian communities know your saving grace and abundant mercy, and may they all be places of hope and reconciliation.

We pray for families. Forgive the sins committed in the name of love, because of our fear and need for control. We pray for those who find abuse, neglect and cruelty within their own homes. May they find a voice and a place of comfort and safety where healing can begin.

We pray for world leaders and governments. Forgive the sins committed in the name of political expediency because of our need for power. We pray for those who suffer under unjust and repressive regimes. May they find courage and strength and may all leaders learn to govern with integrity and honesty.

We pray for our world. Forgive the sins committed in the name of greed because of our selfishness. We pray for those places where there is not enough food or clean drinking water. We remember those who seek to bring relief to populations on the brink of starvation. Motivate all of us, people and governments, to contribute to the answers and not just complain about the problems.

Holy God, hear us and renew us.
We pray in the name of him who lived, died and rose again that we might know forgiveness and freedom, our Lord Jesus Christ.
Amen.

Dedication:

Holy God, we go from this place forgiven and free,
knowing your peace goes with us. **Amen.**

MOTHERING SUNDAY

Intercessions:

Almighty God, guide us by your Spirit to pray as you ask.

We bring our prayers on this Mothering Sunday, and consider the mixed blessing of being a parent in today's society. We admit our confusion and uncertainty when we think about 'mother'. We expect so much, and hold such high ideals about what a mother should be. Yet experience tells us those expectations and ideals are often unrealistic and impossible to attain.

We pray for those women who reflect the best qualities
    of motherhood.
Those who truly seek to raise their children in a loving and
    safe environment.
Those who give of themselves to ensure their children
    are nurtured.
Those who seem to be possessed of an ability to make mothering
    appear effortless.
Those, who though not perfect, try hard to seek the best
    for their children.
We give thanks for such women, we stand in awe of their skills and abilities and we pray for them. May they know the value of what they do, may they be supported in their task and may they be able to share those skills with others.

We pray for women who struggle with the task of mothering.
Those who are, or who feel, inadequate.
Those whose parenting skills are less than they could be.
Those who struggle to do the best they can with little help
    or support.
Those who do not understand how to be a good mother because
    of a lack of good models or any training.
We want to understand how it is for them, we empathise with their difficulties and we pray for them. May they not be afraid to find and ask for help, and may they find support not judgment and condemnation.

We pray for women who long to be mothers but cannot.
Those whose circumstances make motherhood impossible.
Those who know, or are discovering they are infertile.
Those who will need medical intervention if they are
    to become pregnant.
We want to understand how it is for them, we empathise with
their struggles and we pray for them. May they learn to adapt to
the reality of their situation, may they mourn the loss of what
might have been and find places where they can express the hurt
they carry.

We pray for women who have hurt their children.
Those who have hurt their children physically or emotionally.
Those who have hurt their children intentionally
    or unintentionally.
Those who do not know how much their words and actions
    wound their children.
We want to understand how it is for them, we empathise with
their situations and we pray for them. May they find new ways of
mothering and relating to their children, and ways to heal the
wounds inflicted in ignorance and anger. May there be people
who can guide them and show them healthier ways to look after
their children.

We pray for women who live apart from their children.
Those who are separated because of divorce.
Those who choose to allow someone else to raise their children
    because they cannot.
Those who have had their children taken away by any agency.
Those who are estranged from their children by family argument.
Those whose child has chosen to run away.
We want to understand how it is for them, we empathise with
their struggles and we pray for them. May they find some hope
that the future will be different, and may there be those who can
work with them toward reconciliation.

Almighty God, we bring our prayers in the name of him who truly
understands and knows what it is to be a parent in today's world,
our Lord and Saviour, Jesus Christ.
Amen.

PALM SUNDAY

Collect:

Lord God, coming as Redeemer, riding a donkey,
the crowd's words, 'Hosanna to the son of David!'
ringing in your ears,
come to us in this time of worship
move us by your Holy Spirit to sing your praises
that we might go from this place
with a renewed sense of your redeeming love.
Through Jesus Christ our Lord. **Amen.**

Confession:

Lord God, coming as Redeemer,
riding into our lives, offering forgiveness and new beginnings.
Help us to accept the forgiveness and new life you offer,
to all who come in penitence and faith.

We confess the lost opportunities when we have failed you,
    ourselves and other people.
We confess the lost opportunities when we have betrayed you,
    ourselves and other people.
We confess the lost opportunities when we have denied you,
    ourselves and other people.

Lord God, coming as Redeemer,
forgive us, cleanse us and restore us,
for we ask it in the name of our precious Redeemer,
Jesus Christ our Lord. **Amen.**

Praise and Thanksgiving:

Lord God, coming as Redeemer,
riding into our lives, with love,
Help us to worship you as you deserve.
Help us to thank you as you deserve.

Lord God, our Father, for your providential care, and
    for your gracious love:
We give you thanks and praise

Lord God, Jesus the Son, for your redeeming activity,
   and for your loving concern:
We give you thanks and praise

Lord God, Holy Spirit, for your comforting, for your guidance and
   for your empowering presence.
We give you thanks and praise

Lord God, coming as Redeemer,
riding into our lives, with love,
we worship you, we adore you,
we give you thanks and praise
in the Spirit's power,
through our precious Redeemer,
Jesus Christ our Lord. **Amen.**

Intercessions:

Lord God, coming as Redeemer,
riding into our lives with a call
to pray for the needs of others,
We pray for people everywhere
according to their need.

(silence)

We pray for your Church, the body of Christ.
The local church where we worship and know the people.
The church down the street, whose people we do not know
   so well.
The churches throughout the world known and unknown to us.
May your Holy Spirit dwell in all churches, in all leaders, in all
members, motivating each person to seek your will for their lives
and enabling each one to serve you in the place you have called
them to be.

We pray for government, for those who lead civic affairs.
The local government of this community.
The national government of this country.
The governments throughout the world that we know
   so little about.
May your Holy Spirit dwell in all governments, in all leaders, in
all members motivating each person to seek your way of justice,
enabling all people to live as you intend us to live.

We pray for those who are ill, or troubled.
Those known to us, people from this community,
    our families and friends.
Those who are struggling to make sense of faith.
Those who are searching for some meaning to life.
May your Holy Spirit dwell in each one, motivating each person to
seek for healing and wholeness, enabling them to be sustained in
this time of difficulty.

Lord God, coming as Redeemer,
accept our prayers
and help us to seek to be involved in the answers.
Through Jesus Christ our Redeemer.
Amen.

Dedication:

Lord God, coming as Redeemer,
riding into our lives
with a call to worship and service,
go with us from this place.
Give to us your courage, your grace and your love,
as we seek to serve you in the world.
Through Jesus Christ our Redeemer.
Amen.

MAUNDY THURSDAY

Collect:

'This do in remembrance of me.' Father God, we come in remembrance of our Lord Jesus Christ who gave himself freely for us. As we gather in remembrance, come to us again, that we might find in this time of worship a fresh touch of your Spirit and a fresh knowledge of the price Jesus paid for our freedom. For it is in his name and to his praise and glory that we gather. **Amen.**

Praise:

God, you are awesome and wonderful
creating and redeeming us,
sending your Son for our salvation
offering forgiveness and a new beginning to all who come.

We adore you

God, you are awesome and wonderful
sustaining and renewing us,
sending your Holy Spirit for our comfort
offering strength and a guiding hand to all who come.

We adore you

God, you are awesome and wonderful
calling and equipping us,
sending your Son as our example
offering your love and grace to all who come.

We adore you

God, you are awesome and wonderful
moving and challenging us,
sending your Holy Spirit for our encouragement
offering the assurance of your presence to all who come.

We adore you

God, you are awesome and wonderful.
We worship and adore you.
Through Jesus Christ our Lord.
Amen.

Confession:

Lord Jesus, you left us these things, bread and wine
simple reminders of yourself and your work.
In your body and blood is our salvation, forgiveness for our sins.
We are here, remembering your death and resurrection, knowing
you are willing and able to forgive us when we come in faith and
trust.

Forgive us that we so quickly forget your ways.
You have taught us about peace,
    and we have chosen war. Forgive us.
You have taught us about love,
    and we have chosen hate. Forgive us.
You have taught us about mercy,
    and we have chosen injustice. Forgive us.
You have taught us to remember,
    and we have chosen to forget. Forgive us.
Forgive us that we so quickly forget your ways.
In your body and blood is our forgiveness and restoration,
    and we thank you
Lord Jesus Christ.
Amen.

Intercessions:

Lord, you have set us an example of sacrificial giving; you have
shown us how we should serve one another. Yet so often we
strive to be takers, rather than givers. We are uncomfortable
with the role of servant. We do not like to be the one who washes
another's feet. Like the disciples of long ago, so often we hold
back, waiting for someone else to take on the role of servant.
Aware of our inclination to avoid servanthood, we come asking
for forgiveness, for ourselves and for the world. We bring our
concerns for your Church and the world.

Lord, you are a servant; teach us to be servants too

Lord, you have set us an example; you have shown us how we
should treat one another. Your Church, your Body, has failed to
be a servant. We pray for the Church throughout the world.
May she truly learn the way of servanthood. May all church
communities be places of servants seeking to do your will with
grace and humility, and a proper sense of your Lordship.

Lord, you are a servant; teach us to be servants too

Lord, you have set us an example; you have shown us how we should treat one another. Yet in so many situations and places people relate to one another with greed, with grasping, with violence, with hatred, with oppression and injustice. We pray for people throughout the world who are in positions of leadership and responsibility. May they know the way of servanthood. May all who hold political and monetary power use that power to serve with integrity those for whom they are responsible.

Lord, you are a servant; teach us to be servants too

Lord, you have set us an example; you have shown us how we should treat one another. Yet in many places people are arrested, detained, imprisoned, tortured, killed, because their skin is the wrong colour. Because their faith is the wrong kind. Because their political beliefs are different to those of the ruling government. Because they are willing to speak out against injustice. We pray for an end to such practices, and for a willingness on our part to change the situations in which such abuses can occur.

Lord, you are a servant; teach us to be servants too

Lord, you have set us an example, you have shown us how we should treat one another. We pray for all people, that we will learn to treat each other with respect, and with tolerance. Send your Holy Spirit, Lord, change our hearts and give us courage to work for a world in which justice, and integrity are the norm.

Lord, you are a servant; teach us to be servants too

In the name of him who came to show us the way of servanthood, our Lord Jesus Christ.
Amen.

GOOD FRIDAY

Thanksgiving:

Eternal God,
we give you thanks that
you did not leave us in our sin
but sent your Son that we might know
your forgiveness.

God the Father, we thank you for sending the Son.
God the Son, Jesus our Lord, we thank you for your life,
    death and resurrection.
God the Spirit, we thank you for drawing us always
    to repentance.

Accept our thanksgiving, offered in the name of our Lord Jesus
Christ. **Amen**.

Confession:

Lord God,
on the cross we see your outstretched arms of love
drawing all people to yourself.
As we contemplate your death for us
we are aware of our sins.

Forgive us our apathy and avoidance.
You have set us an example of sacrificial love
    and we sidestep your call.
Forgive us our selfishness and self-centredness.
You have set us an example of sacrificial love
    and we sidestep your demands.
Forgive us our blindness and deafness.
You have set us an example of sacrificial love
    and we sidestep your grace.

Loving God, forgive us, we pray, for all these things. Help us to
listen to your call and follow your example of sacrificial love, for
the sake of him who loved us enough to die for us, our Lord
Jesus Christ.
Amen.

Intercessions:

Brothers and sisters in Christ, let us bring our cares and concerns to the foot of the cross.

We remember before you, O Lord, your Church, the Body of Christ on earth. May she shine with the light of your love and fulfil her calling to be a community of forgiveness and reconciliation.

At your cross, Lord, we find strength to follow you

We remember before you, O Lord, all world leaders and people in positions of authority. May they know right from wrong and fulfil their calling to serve others with strength and sensitivity.

At your cross, Lord, we find strength to follow you

We remember before you, O Lord, those who are ill in body, mind or spirit. Those who struggle to make sense of the world in the light of their faith in you. Those who have lost their faith in you. Those who know they are dying and those who wait with them. Those who grieve. May they know the support of family and friends in times of difficulty and distress, and fulfil their calling to be who they are.

At your cross, Lord, we find strength to follow you

We remember before you, O Lord, all people in this community. The minister, church stewards, Junior Church teachers, pastoral visitors, worship leaders and stewards of our property and finance. We remember all who come to worship and all who are no longer able to attend due to age or infirmity. May we be refreshed by your Spirit and fulfil our calling to follow you.

At your cross, Lord, we find strength to follow you

We bring our prayers in the name of him who fulfilled his calling that we might know our sins are forgiven, our Lord and Saviour, Jesus Christ.
Amen.

EASTER DAY

Adoration:

We rejoice today in the obedience of Jesus who went to the cross, emerging triumphant, victor over sin and death.

He is risen, alleluia!

We rejoice today in the witness of the disciples who proclaimed:

He is risen, alleluia!

We rejoice today in men and women who through the ages
have risked all to spread the gospel.

He is risen, alleluia!

We rejoice today in the Holy Spirit who enables us to be proclaimers of Good News.

He is risen, alleluia!

Eternal God, we rejoice today in the resurrection of your Son – fulfilling your purpose on the cross – leaving your Spirit to comfort and guide.

He is risen, alleluia!

We come in praise and adoration,
rejoicing in all that you have done for us
Through Jesus Christ our Lord.
Amen.

Confession:

Rejoicing in your triumph over death and sin,
    we recognise our own sinfulness.
We also recognise your loving mercy and know you freely forgive
    all who are truly sorry.

Forgive us the sins of thought, of word, and of action.

(*silence*)

Forgive us the sins of commission and omission.

(*silence*)

Forgive us the sins that destroy your Body on earth and those that build walls between us.

(*silence*)

In the name of Jesus forgive us, we pray, that we might know the freedom Jesus died to bring to us, and that we might continue to serve you in the world. **Amen**.

Intercessions:

Brothers and sisters in Christ, in the name of our risen Lord Jesus, let us bring our prayers for the needs of all people to our heavenly Father.

We pray for all Christian leaders, ministers, preachers and teachers of your gospel. May they rejoice in the good news of salvation and proclaim the risen Lord faithfully. Bless each one of them, that they may be a blessing to others.

Risen Lord; hear us, renew us, send us out

We pray for all doctors, nurses and emergency workers. May they rejoice in the skills you have given which enable them to bring hope, healing and wholeness to those in their care. May they also know guidance and support in the times of pain and frustration when their skills are not enough to prevent permanent injury, disability or death. Bless each one of them, that they may be a blessing to others.

Risen Lord; hear us, renew us, send us out

We pray for all people who are suffering today in any way, especially for those who are imprisoned because of political or religious belief. Those who are tortured, physically and emotionally. Those who now must live with the knowledge that death is not far away. Those in the midst of war, or famine. Those who are ill in body or mind. And those who struggle as they watch a loved one suffer. May they be conscious of the support of family and friends and may they find courage to face their suffering with dignity and a sense of self-worth. Bless each one of them, that they may be a blessing to others.

Risen Lord; hear us, renew us, send us out

We pray for our local community. For those in places of influence and those who wield power. Our local MP (*name*) and those who serve on the city/town council. Those who are responsible for the education of our children. And those who are responsible for upholding our our laws. May each one serve to the best of their ability according to your ways of justice and peace. May they also know help and friendship when the tasks before them are difficult or painful. Bless each one of them, that they may be a blessing to others.

Risen Lord; hear us, renew us, send us out

We pray for the Methodist Church. For the President (*name*) and Vice-President (*name*) of Conference. For all decision making bodies that decide Church policy. The chairman of this district (*name*). The superintendent (*name*) and ministers of this circuit. May each one find joy and a sense of peace as they serve you in this particular way. May they find wise counsel and spiritual guidance in times of dryness and emptiness. Bless each one of them, that they may be a blessing to others.

Risen Lord; hear us, renew us, send us out

Risen Lord, we bring our prayers in your name, knowing our heavenly Father delights to hear our concerns.
Amen.

ASCENSION DAY

Collect:

Almighty God, as we celebrate the ascension of your Son, we know he has not left us alone but sent his Holy Spirit to empower us. Help us by that same Spirit to put our trust in your presence. Through Jesus Christ our Lord. **Amen**.

Praise:

Almighty God, we praise you for your power

When the disciples thought it was the end, that Jesus was dead, your power raised him to life.

Almighty God, we praise you for your power

While the disciples watched in wonder, your power enabled Jesus to return to you.

Almighty God, we praise you for your power

When the disciples worried about the future, your power sent the Holy Spirit as comforter and guide.

Almighty God, we praise you for your power

Through our risen and ascended Lord, Jesus Christ.
Amen.

Confession:

Almighty God, the ascension of our Lord Jesus reminds us of your power, your presence and your love. We know in the light of those things that we are sinful people in need of your grace. We come humbly confessing our sins, knowing your grace is sufficient. In silence we bring our personal confession to you.

(*silence*)

Almighty God, forgive us our sins and fill us with true thankfulness for all your goodness to us. In the name of our risen and ascended Lord, Jesus. **Amen.**

Dedication:

Risen and ascended Lord, we give you thanks, and we offer ourselves afresh to your work. Fill us again and again. Bless us with a sense of the intensity of your love for us, so filled with that love we may be able to rise to the full maturity of faith. In your name we ask it. **Amen.**

Intercessions:

Almighty God, the ascension of Jesus confirms him as your Son, and reminds us that for the Spirit to come and dwell among us, he had to take his place at your right hand. As we pray in the power of the Spirit, we know that Jesus is interceding for us. Almighty God, risen and ascended Lord, Holy Spirit, hear us and help us.

There are many needs throughout the world about which we
    are concerned.
Some situations we know about through personal involvement.
Some situations we know about through reading newspapers.
Some situations we know about because of the images on
    our televisions.
It is hard for us, Lord God, because we know there is a limit to the situations we can respond to personally. As we pray, help us to know what we can do.

Almighty God, risen and ascended Lord, Holy Spirit, hear us and help us

We pray for those situations in which we are personally involved,: especially we pray for the people, events and places in our minds and on our hearts today.

(silence)

Almighty God, risen and ascended Lord, Holy Spirit, hear us and help us

We pray for those situations we know about from our newspapers: especially we pray for . . . and all the people, events and places unknown, yet in our minds and on our hearts today.

(silence)

Almighty God, risen and ascended Lord, Holy Spirit, hear us and help us

We pray for those situations we know about from our televisions: especially we pray for . . . and all the people, events and places unknown, yet in our minds and on our hearts today.

(*silence*)

Almighty God, risen and ascended Lord, Holy Spirit, hear us and help us

Almighty God, risen and ascended Lord, Holy Spirit, hear our prayers for the world, offered in your powerful name.
Amen.

PENTECOST

Praise:

Today and always, Father God
we offer you our thanks and praise.
Especially today we praise and worship you
because you have not left us alone
but sent the Holy Spirit.

The Holy Spirit comes to us
as a rushing wind
and as tongues of fire,
and we are full of awe and wonder.
Holy Spirit, energy of God,
prodding, challenging, provoking and comforting
we worship and adore you.

Take hold of us again, Holy Spirit; help us to be receptive to your
coming, that we might worship and adore our heavenly Father in
spirit and in truth.
In the precious name of Jesus we pray. **Amen**.

Confession:

Lord God, your Spirit convicts us of our sin.
We know the times we have chosen the destructive path
    the times we have chosen our own way
    the times we have ignored your demands
    the times we have deliberately disobeyed you
    the times we have been childish and self-centred.

Lord God, your Spirit convicts us of our sin.
Come, Holy Spirit; breathe on us with the forgiveness and
renewal the Father offers to all who are truly sorry.
In the precious name of Jesus we pray. **Amen**.

Thanksgiving:

Father, in so many ways and for so many things
    we are truly thankful.
We are thankful for all your gifts and your constant presence
    in our lives.
Today we give thanks for the Holy Spirit.

For all those who through the ages have been empowered by
your Spirit to follow you.
For all those who through the ages have been comforted by
your Spirit in times of distress and difficulty.
For all those who through the ages have been equipped by
your Spirit for worship and service.
For all those who through the ages have been filled by
your Spirit for some special task.
For all those who through the ages have been encouraged by
your Spirit to see the impossible.
For all those who through the ages have been led by your Spirit
to challenge injustice and apathy.
We give you thanks for the gift of the Holy Spirit.

May we be empowered by that same Spirit,
May we be open to his coming,
May we with thankful hearts be filled again
and be made ready for the task of following Jesus.

For it is in his precious name and for his sake we pray.
Amen.

Intercessions:

In the power of the Spirit, Father God, we come,
bringing a world in need of renewal.
Hear us as we pray and let your Spirit breathe on us.

Holy Spirit, breathe your renewing strength on all who struggle
with hardships and difficulties.

People in war-torn areas of the world; people maimed, disabled,
made homeless or killed as a result of war.
People in areas of the world where food and water are scarce,
where people suffer disease and illness as a result of poor
sanitation and lack of cleanliness.
People who are tortured and abused for their faith in you, or
because they do not subscribe to the ruling political ideology.

**Come, Holy Spirit, breathe on them and us, bringing your
strength**

Holy Spirit, breathe your renewing courage on all who struggle with hardships and difficulties.

People who are physically ill, in hospital or at home
People who care for a loved one who is sick or dying
People who are suffering in the mind the terrors and torments of
    internal distress.
People who are suffering spiritually, their faith in you fading.

Come, Holy Spirit, breathe on them and us, bringing your courage

Holy Spirit, breathe your renewing love on all who struggle with hardships and difficulties.

People who are facing hard decisions, especially those in
    this community.
People who are contemplating self-destructive acts
People who are consumed by guilt over their actions
People who are convinced they are unlovable and unworthy.

Come, Holy Spirit, breathe on them and us, bringing your love

In the power of the Spirit, Father God, and in the name of Jesus, send your Holy Spirit into this needy world and renew us with strength, courage and love.
Amen.

Dedication:

Come, Holy Spirit
refresh us with your wind
relight us with your fire
blow on us and through us
as we go forth in Jesus' name
to serve God in the world.
Amen.

REMEMBRANCE SUNDAY

Intercessions:

God our Father, on this day of remembrance we bring our prayers, trusting in your unfailing love.

God our Father, on this day of remembrance we think about war and its effects. We remember wars of the past, the people involved, the pain and loss caused and the ongoing legacy for those who fought, those who lost loved ones and those who still struggle physically and emotionally.

God our Father, we don't understand
Help us to trust in your unfailing love

God our Father, on this day of remembrance we think about war and its effects. We remember present wars, the people involved, the people who have lost family, friends and homes, and those who struggle physically and emotionally.

God our Father, we don't understand
Help us to trust in your unfailing love

God our Father, on this day of remembrance we pray for peace. We remember individuals at war with themselves. We remember people at war with family and neighbours. Nations at war with themselves. Nation at war with nation. We ask for peace. Your peace. A lasting peace that will show each of us how we can live in harmony, settling our differences without resorting to violence.

God our Father, we don't understand
Help us to trust in your unfailing love

God our Father, on this day of remembrance we think about peace. We commit ourselves afresh to working for peace in all situations. Motivate each one of us to right actions that we might know true peace.

God our Father, we don't understand
Help us to trust in your unfailing love

God our Father, on this day of remembrance we think about your Son, Jesus, who came to show us your way of peace. In him we pray for an end to fighting and conflict and war.
In the name of Jesus who gives us his peace.
Amen.

CHRISTIAN UNITY

Intercessions:

Lord God, we bring our prayers for the unity of your Church.
We pray for our brothers and sisters in Christ,
that, transformed by your grace, we might learn from each other
and grow in understanding.

Lord God, forgive us, we pray,
where we have been fearful and hesitant
where we have been suspicious and intolerant
where we have been anxious and insecure

(*silence*)

transform our lives by your grace that we might bear witness to
your reconciling love.

Lord God, we pray for all Christians,
those known to us, in our own church,
in the churches of this neighbourhood
in the churches across the world about which we know so little,
and for all leaders of our churches,
that, transformed by your grace, we may work together in your
kingdom.

Lord God, we pray for ecumenical projects, locally and nationally
especially those known to us,
that, transformed by your grace, they may be living examples of
reconciliation and cooperation.

Lord God, we pray that in openness and honesty,
transformed by your grace,
we will learn to respect and value our brothers and sisters
    in Christ
and not allow denominational labels to divide us.

Lord God, we pray that you will challenge our apathy,
disturb our comfortable existence
and transform us by your grace to be more than we are,
to see the world and our place in it through your eyes.

Lord God, we pray for a renewed enthusiasm
     for our work together,
transform us by your grace,
that we might see our difference as God given, a gift for the good
of the whole body of Christ.

Lord God, in Jesus' name we pray. **Amen.**

WORLD LEPROSY DAY

Intercessions:

Heavenly Father, today we remember the work of the Leprosy Mission and pray for those who live with the effects of this disease. There is still ignorance about leprosy, and fear, intolerance and unjust treatment of those who suffer. Help us to be involved, to gain knowledge, and to challenge unjust practices. Help us to respond in practical ways to support this work and those who bring much needed help and service to those who contract leprosy.

We pray for the work of the Leprosy Offices and for:
> the executive director
> those whose job is fund-raising
> those responsible for publicity
> the secretarial workers
> the volunteers
> the workers who are sent out.

We thank you for the years of work since the Mission's founding in 1874, that has enabled us to say that leprosy is now curable, and that many of the effects can be alleviated by various treatments.

We pray for those:
> who work in Africa, Asia and Europe, bringing vaccines that help to cure the disease and prevent or alleviate disability.
> whose job it is to train local people to become paramedics or non-medical supervisors.
> whose task it is to educate people, dispelling their ignorance and fear.
> who fight the injustice and prejudice, bringing a better quality of life to people struck by this disease.

We thank you for those who are prepared to do this work, and we ask that they will find support, encouragement and a sense of a job well done.

We pray for those :
> who live with the physical effects of leprosy
> who live with the social effects
> who live with the ignorance and fear

who will need surgery
who will need special shoes or a prosthesis
who will need rehabilitation
who need equipment and supplies
who have lost jobs or families.

We pray that there will always be all that is needed to bring fullness of life.

Father God, you call us to respond to need, to proclaim your gospel of love in word and deed. We cannot be the whole answer, but we can respond. Help us to give of our time, our prayers and our financial support, that leprosy might become a thing of the past.

In Jesus' name we pray, and for his sake. **Amen**.

EDUCATION SUNDAY

Intercessions:

Father God, in the power of the Holy Spirit we bring our concerns and worries about education and all people involved in this work.

Father God, we give you thanks for:
our education system
all teachers
all who work in education
the joys of teaching.

We pray that all who are involved will use their skills wisely, feel themselves to be valued and help the students in their care to learn and grow.

Father God, we remember the work of teachers, the men and women who have trained hard, and now use their skills in educating others. We acknowledge their work, and we want to understand the joys, the stresses and the strains they feel in their daily work.

Father God, we pray for:
dedicated teachers
teachers who feel inadequate or stressed.

Lord God, we remember all these people in their various tasks; give them strength, courage and a sense of purpose in teaching

Father God, we pray for:
struggling or unsupported teachers
teachers who feel overwhelmed by their workload.

Lord God, we remember all these people in their various tasks; give them peace, joy and a sense of purpose in teaching

Father God, we pray for teachers in:
    special needs schools
    infant and junior schools
    secondary schools
    colleges and universities
    adult education.

Lord God, we remember all these people in their various tasks; give them energy, commitment and a sense of purpose in their work

Father God, we pray for:
    schools learning how to be responsible for their own budgets.
    governors learning how best to support and motivate school workers.
    head teachers trying to motivate themselves and others.
    teachers whom we know personally.

Lord God, we remember all these people in their various tasks; give them awareness, sensitivity and a sense of purpose in their work

Father God, we pray for:
    people training to be teachers
    people considering a career in education.

Lord God, we remember all these people in their various situations, give them a clear sense of direction

Lord God, we know that teaching can be a thankless task. Help us to be aware of the needs of those who have the responsibility for educating others. May we as a community be supportive and caring, offering a listening ear and practical concern whenever we can.

Through Jesus Christ our Lord. **Amen**.

FATHER'S DAY

Intercessions:

Lord God, we bring our prayers for the needs of others, and today we concentrate our thoughts on fathers.

Jesus has taught us to call you Father, daddy. For some of us that is a hard thing to do, for even the best of earthly fathers fall far short of your heavenly ideal. We have clear images of how fathers should behave and act, and yet so often the reality does not match the image. There is confusion and doubt in our society, for men who do not know how they can possibly live up to the ideal, and for children who experience fathers as absent or abusive.

We pray for fathers, for those:
> who display the best qualities of fatherhood
> who work hard at parenting, often in difficult situations
> who seem to have a natural ability to be good fathers
> who seem to reflect your fatherhood.

Father God, the model for all fathers, bless them

We pray for fathers, for those:
> who are abusive toward their children
> who do not know how to be good fathers
> who are separated from their children by divorce or
> imprisonment or choice
> who deny their responsibilities and fail to support their
> children, emotionally or financially.

Father God, the model for all fathers, help them

We pray for fathers, for those:
> who are good models of fatherhood
> who have the ability to love
> who have the ability to laugh
> who are reliable.

Father God, the model for all fathers, bless them

We pray for fathers, for those:
>who do not understand how important their task is
>who have lost the ability to care for their children
>who have been denied the presence of a good father in their own lives
>who have given up on themselves and their children.

Father God, the model for all fathers, help them

Father God, accept our prayers, and help us, in spite of the mixed experience we have of earthly fathers, to accept your fathering, for we ask it in the name of your precious Son, Jesus Christ. **Amen.**

HARVEST

Collect:

Lord God, we acknowledge your creative power in nature and life as we celebrate harvest. Fill us with thankfulness for all your gifts and help us to share in your creative activity. Through Jesus Christ our Lord. **Amen**.

Thanksgiving:

Lord God, we acknowledge your creative power and energy and we thank you for harvest-time.

For the seasons: winter, spring, summer, autumn, that come and go each in their turn.

Creator God, we give you thanks

For the rain and the sun, helping us grow the food we need, and the trees, flowers and plants that sustain life and add to the beauty of the world.

Creator God, we give you thanks

For the harvest of the land, for fruit and vegetables, for the harvest of the seas, for the harvest of earth, minerals and coal.

Creator God, we give you thanks.

For the balance of nature, the rhythms of life, the ebb and flow of the world as we know it.

Creator God, we give you thanks.

For the technology that makes our lives easier, for the work of industries, and for the work of the emergency services.

Creator God, we give you thanks.

Creator God, we give you thanks and praise, through Jesus Christ our Lord. **Amen**.

Confession:

Lord God, as we acknowledge your creative power and energy, we confess our own destructiveness.
We destroy the earth and all it provides for us
We destroy each other in our conflicts and wars
We destroy by our greed and selfishness
We destroy by our words of anger and hate
We destroy by our actions and behaviour.

Creator God, forgive us, and enable us to follow your example of creativity, that we might live together in harmony with nature and each other.

Through Jesus Christ our Lord. **Amen**.

Intercessions:

Lord God, we acknowledge your creative power and energy, bringing our prayers for a world in need of your creativity.

Creator God, hear us, renew us, help us

Lord God, we pray for your Church throughout the world. May there be a harvest of freedom, places where your Spirit moves in and through us, your people, that we might be all that you call us to be.

Creator God, hear us, renew us, help us

Lord God, we pray for this earth. May there continue to be a harvest of land and sea. May the people who work to bring our daily food continue to use their skill and patience and know the value of the work they do.

Creator God, hear us, renew us, help us

Lord God, we pray for the areas of the world where the harvest has failed. For places where lack of rain has ruined the crops. For places where war and conflict has prevented the planting of crops. For places where there is hunger and famine. May those who work to bring relief and aid continue their work and know that it is essential. May governments be moved to offer support that will enable people to take responsibility for their own future.

Creator God, hear us, renew us, help us

Lord God, we pray for those who work in all manner of places and situations. For those in industry. For those who develop our technology. For those who work in the emergency services. For those responsible for upholding laws and keeping peace. May they know the importance of the tasks in which they are involved and may they find strength and support as they seek to contribute to society.

Creator God, hear us, renew us, help us

Lord God, we pray for those who are unemployed. For people who have been unemployed for many years and have lost any hope of gaining employment. For those who have lost any sense of self-esteem. For those who are in a state of shock, having been made redundant recently. May they find ways to value themselves and may we as a society learn not to value people only by the occupation they perform. Help us to value people for who they are and not what they do.

Creator God, hear us, renew us, help us

Lord God, we pray for those whose work is not paid. For those who take time out from a career to raise children. For those who cannot accept paid employment because they are caring for a sick or disabled relative. For those who work in a voluntary capacity, in the health service, in prisons, in community care, churches and charitable organisations. May they fulfil the task they are called to do and give of their best in each situation. May we as a society value the work they do as they contribute to our lives.

Creator God, hear us, renew us, help us

Lord God, we acknowledge your creative power and energy and we bring these prayers in the name of Jesus Christ our Lord. Creator God, hear us, renew us and send us out to live and work in your name.
Amen.

RACIAL JUSTICE SUNDAY

Intercessions:

Almighty God, our Heavenly Father, on Racial Justice Sunday we bring our prayers and concerns to you. Guide us as we pray, that we might be part of the solution, not contributors to the problem.

Lord God, we pray for our churches, places that are supposed to welcome everyone, regardless of their skin colour or social standing.
We know that there is racism and racial disadvantage in our churches.
We ask you to forgive us, and help us find ways to move forward, ways that will enable all people to be accepted and valued as they are.
Help us to listen to those who experience prejudice and racism.
Help us to be informed and to fight against injustice wherever and whenever we can.
Lord of all, hear our prayer

Lord God, we pray for our society, aware of the racism to which we have contributed knowingly and unknowingly.
We ask you to forgive us.
Help us to be aware of the experiences of ethnic groups in our society, that we might become a society that is open to diversity and that values different cultures, working together rather than in opposition.
Help us to be socially and politically aware.
Help us to use our knowledge to work for a society that is just and free of oppression.
Lord of all, hear our prayer

Lord God, we pray for other countries, where racism and disadvantage is rife, for regimes under which ideologies are based on the superiority of one race over another.
We ask you to forgive us for our contribution to such regimes.
Help us to challenge racism in all its forms, at home and abroad.
Help us to be aware, to pray and not give up the dream of racial equality.
Lord of all, hear our prayer

Lord, we pray for our churches and our society.
We ask you to forgive us for our insensitivity and ignorance.
Help us to examine our language.
Help us to be aware of words, phrases and types of behaviour
    that are offensive and hurtful.
Help us to be aware of how racism operates in our culture.

Lord of all, hear our prayer

Lord God, we pray for people who have experienced racism.
For people who have lost a job because of the colour of their skin.
People who have been taunted.
Children who have been teased and ostracised.
People who have been physically beaten or tortured because of
    their race.
People who live in fear.
People who feel paralysed by their experiences.
Forgive us our blindness and apathy.
Help us to face the reality of racism and work together
    for change.

Lord of all, hear our prayer

Almighty God, you created each one of us
    and you delight in variety.
Help us to celebrate that variety as we seek to serve you
    in the world.

Through Jesus Christ our Lord.
Amen.

WORLD AIDS DAY

Lord God, we bring our worries, fears and concerns about HIV infection and AIDS. We know there is much misunderstanding and prejudice among people about this disease. We pray that we will make time to become informed, so that we might stand firm against such prejudice, misunderstanding and misinformation.

Lord God, we pray for those who work in the area of research. May they be strengthened and encouraged in their task, continue to learn more about this disease and work toward a cure.

Lord God, we pray for governments, that they will show a greater willingness to make funds available for research and education.

Lord God, we pray for all who work with people living with AIDS or HIV infection. For doctors, nurses and counsellors. May they show sensitivity to their patients' needs and help individuals and families come to terms with the life-threatening nature of this infection.

Lord God, we pray for men, women and children who know they are HIV positive or have AIDS. May they find encouragement and hope as they learn to live fully with this complex disease. May they find support and understanding from family, friends and society.

Lord God, we pray for people afraid to be tested because of the ignorance and prejudice of society. Give them the courage they need to seek for wholeness of life.

Lord God, we pray for people afraid because of ignorance and prejudice. For those who have lost jobs, homes, family and friends because they are HIV positive or have AIDS. Help all of us to learn the truth about this disease, to fight against ignorance and prejudice and be open to the pain and vulnerability of others.

Lord God, we pray for people watching a loved one struggle with the effects of this illness. Help them find strength for the task of loving and supporting.

Lord God, we remember those who have died. And we remember the loved ones who mourn their loss. Let them find comfort, peace and hope as they struggle with the pain of loss and death.

Lord God, you sent your Son, Jesus, that we might find wholeness and forgiveness. When we have been afraid because of our own ignorance or prejudice, forgive us. When we have turned from the need of another because of our own fears, forgive us. When we have closed our hearts and minds to the pain this disease brings, forgive us.

Renew each of us, that together we might seek for that wholeness of life Jesus died to bring.

Lord God, accept our prayers in the name of Jesus Christ, our Lord and Saviour.
Amen.

Prayers for the Connexion and other organisations

START OF THE CONNEXIONAL YEAR

Collect:

Almighty God, as we worship, we reach out to you, knowing you seek always to reach out to us. Let us find a fresh sense of vision, a fresh understanding of your word to us, a fresh will to serve you, through Jesus Christ our Lord. **Amen.**

Praise and Thanksgiving:

Almighty God, we give you thanks and praise,
You are our creator and Redeemer.

For your powerful word, reaching out to all people everywhere:

We give you thanks and praise

For your active word, seeking out all whom you love:

We give you thanks and praise

For your redemptive word, forgiving all who truly repent:

We give you thanks and praise

Almighty God, your Word is life for us. We give you thanks and praise, through your powerful, active, redeeming Word, Jesus Christ, our Lord and Saviour. **Amen.**

Confession:

Almighty God, we come in repentance, aware of the ways in which we have denied your Word and chosen our own way.
We confess that so often we have ignored your Word:
    we have taken for granted the freedom we enjoy in worship
    we have taken for granted the easy availability of your Word
    we read your Word, and yet do not obey.

Almighty God, forgive us, help us to hear and heed your words that we might truly be your disciples.
In Jesus' name we pray. **Amen.**

Dedication:

Almighty God, for your living, active, redemptive Word we thank you. We give ourselves again to living your Word in the world. In Jesus' name and in the power of your Holy Spirit. **Amen**.

Intercessions:

Brothers and Sisters in Christ, as a new year begins let us bring our prayers to the Father, prompted by the Holy Spirit and in Jesus' name.

Lord, we pray for all who are in new situations, for:
    probationer ministers, deacons and deaconesses beginning
        their ministry
    ministers who have moved to new churches and circuits
    churches who have welcomed a new minister
    deacons and deaconesses who are beginning in new places
    ministers, deacons and deaconesses who are newly retired.

We pray for all people in these situations that, renewed by your Spirit, they will go forward in faith and trust. Bring to each the talents, gifts and graces they need to work together for your kingdom. Lord, bring your strength, sensitivity and love to bear on all these situations, that each may learn more of what it means to be a community of your people.

Lord, we pray for the Methodist Church, for the people who serve you in so many ways, seeking to share the gospel by word and action, for:
    the President of Conference
    the Vice-President of Conference
    those who work in each of the units of the Church
    all involved in mission, evangelism and outreach
    all involved in social programmes and activities, meeting
        needs in local situations
    all who are beginning their training as ministers,
        deacons or deaconesses
    all who will be giving a year to a Seed Team.

Lord, we pray for all these people that, empowered by your Spirit, they will go forward in faith and trust. Bring to each one fresh strength, and a sense of peace as they grapple with the tasks that lie ahead of them this year. Lord, bring your enabling grace to each of these people and situations, that each may learn more of what it means to be a disciple of Christ.

Lord, we pray for those who are in need or distressed in any way, especially those known to us, for those:
who mourn
who are dying
who are struggling emotionally
who are struggling spiritually
who feel alone
who have lost hope.

Lord, we pray for all these people, that your Holy Spirit would bring encouragement, wholeness and hope. Bring your healing love to bear on these situations, that each may know your sustaining presence.

Lord, there are so many people, places and situations that need our prayers, and we bring some of them to you in the quiet of our hearts, knowing you listen to the things that are important to us.

(*silence*)

Lord, we pray for your presence, guidance and support as we move into the future, trusting in your grace to sustain us whatever may come.

Lord, hear our prayers, for we offer them in the name of Jesus, who always invites us to new beginnings.
Amen.

CONFERENCE

Intercessions:

Retiring President and Vice-President:

Heavenly Father, you call us all to serve you in many different ways. We each have our task in the ongoing work of the mission of your Church. We thank you for those who have served this past year as President (*name*) and Vice-President (*name*) of the Conference.

We thank you for their willingness to serve you and the Church in those tasks.

We thank you for who they are, for their personalities, and their uniqueness.

We pray that you will be with them as they come to the end of this task, enabling them to make the transition from such public work to the more private work of circuit and church life.

May there be for them and their families ongoing support and care as they take time to reflect on the experiences of this past year.

Refresh each of them and give them a fresh touch of your Spirit, that they may find renewal and re-creation.

We offer this our prayer in the name of our Lord and Saviour, Jesus Christ. **Amen**.

Incoming President and Vice-President:

Heavenly Father, you call us all to serve you in many different ways. We each have our task in the ongoing work of the mission of your Church. We thank you for those who will serve this coming year as President (*name*) and Vice-President (*name*) of the Conference.

We thank you for their willingness to serve you and the Church in those tasks.

We thank you for who they are, for their personalities, and their uniqueness.

We pray that your presence will be with them and their families on this journey; that they will know the love, care and prayers of many people, and that we will do our part to help and support them.

Bless them, Lord, that they may be a blessing to the many people they will meet with this year in your name and in the name of the Methodist Church.

Strengthen them for the tasks to come and renew them each day as they give of themselves in time, energy and emotion. Let there be places along the way that will be for them places of rest and re-creation.

We offer our prayer in and through the name of Jesus, the source of our strength. **Amen**.

Ordinands:

Heavenly Father, we remember and pray for those who will be ordained today, as ministers or as deacons *(name any known personally)*.

We remember them and their families on this special occasion.

Be close to each one: ordinands, families and friends, that they may feel your presence and be filled with a sense of the rightness of the task before them.

As they meet in worship, offering themselves to your plan for their lives, strengthen them and give them the courage to face the future with you.

May all who witness these ordinations be aware of your call on their lives and give themselves afresh to your way for them.

Lord, we thank you for those who will be ordained, for their courage and for their willingness to serve you and the Church. Help us to support them with our prayers, our love and our care. Through Jesus Christ our Lord. **Amen**.

Ministerial Session:

Heavenly Father, we remember and pray for the ministerial session of Conference:

for all who have responsibility for its smooth running
for all who work behind the scenes.

Lord, this is your work; help them to do it willingly

for all the work that will be done
for all who will speak
for all who will listen.

Lord, this is your work; help them to do it willingly

for all who will be hosts
for those involved in catering.

Lord, this is your work; help them to do do it willingly

Heavenly Father, in the days of this Conference much will be said and much work will be done. We thank you for those who are involved, offering their time and talents to this important work.
We pray that, as decisions are made and conclusions reached, we will always keep in mind the demands of your gospel and our missionary task in the world in which we live.
We pray that all things will be done for your glory, that we might better serve you, seeking to find new ways to proclaim the good news of the gospel of Jesus Christ.
For it is in his name and for his sake we pray. **Amen**.

Representative Session:

Heavenly Father, we remember and pray for the representative session of Conference:

for all who have responsibility for its smooth running
for all who work behind the scenes.

Lord, this is your work; help them to do it willingly

for all the work that will be done
for all who will speak
for all who will listen.

Lord, this is your work; help them to do it willingly

for all who will be hosts
for those involved in catering.

Lord, this is your work; help them to do do it willingly

Heavenly Father, there is much work to be done, and we thank you for those who are involved in this important task.
We ask that the work will be conducted with openness and honesty and with sensitivity to the diversity among us.
Help us to rejoice in who we are in Christ, and be prepared for the many ways in which we can serve you.
Be with all those who are representatives to this Conference.
Be their wisdom, their strength and their guide.
Let all our decisions in the coming days be made with an awareness of your love for the whole of humanity.
Through Jesus Christ our Lord. **Amen**.

UNIT FOR CHURCH LIFE

Living God, we pray for the life of the Church. You call us to worship and service, to growth and change. We are a family, individuals united by a common bond of love for you and a desire to seek and do your will. In our life together fill us afresh, Lord God, that we might be united in your love, held in your grace, empowered by your Spirit.

We pray for the coordinating secretary; we thank you for *him/her* and *his/her* response to your call to serve the Church in this particular task. We ask that *s/he* will be renewed and strengthened for this work and be courageous in seeking new ways to promote the life of the Church. In our life together fill us afresh, Lord God, that we might be united in your love, held in your grace, empowered by your Spirit.

We pray for the task of Mission.
We remember the work of:
    the commission on evangelism
    the seed teams
    Easter People
    stewardship programmes
    The World Church in Britain
    Grant making policy
    Connexional Advance and Priority Fund Grants
    General Property fund grants
    Home Mission grants
    London Mission grants
    Mission Alongside the Poor grants
    Property Schemes
    Stationing.

Living God, each of these tasks is vital to the ongoing life of your Church; each involves many people.
We pray for all who are involved in these situations that they will be blessed with patience as they seek to lead the Church.

In our life together fill us afresh, Lord God, that we might be united in your love, held in your grace, empowered by your Spirit.

We pray for the study of faith and theology.
We remember the work of:
    Faith and Order
    Apologetics.

Living God, each of these tasks is vital to the ongoing life of your Church; each involves many people. We give you thanks for those in our communities who are blessed with an ability to think deeply about issues of faith and belief. We ask that they will lead us forward with sensitivity and care as we continue to grow in faith, in love and understanding of our Lord Jesus Christ.

In our life together fill us afresh, Lord God, that we might be united in your love, held in your grace, empowered by your Spirit.

We pray for the task of Ministerial Formation.
We remember:
    Individuals who are candidating (*name any known*)
    Those considering a call to presbyteral or diaconal ministry
    Individuals training for presbyteral and diaconal ministries,
        their families and friends. (*name any known*)
    Our theological colleges and courses and the tutors who plan
        and teach there
    The work of ongoing appraisal and further training
    Individuals training as lay workers (*name any known*).

Living God, each of these tasks is vital to the ongoing life of your Church; each involves many people. We give thanks for your continued call to ministry and service, and pray for those who have responded to that call. May they be held by the knowledge that this is your chosen path for their life. We give thanks for those who use their skills and gifts in training others. May they be continually refreshed for their work.

In our life together fill us afresh, Lord God, that we might be united in your love, held in your grace, empowered by your Spirit.

We pray for the task of Pastoral Care and Christian Education.
We remember:
> those who train for and give pastoral care
> those who are becoming church members
> the many Bible study and fellowship groups
> Network
> the Wesley Guilds
> Our children and young people
> Methodist Association of Youth Clubs
> Student Methodist societies
> Regional youth officers
> The Open Learning centre
> The Methodist leadership Racism Awareness Workshops
> World Church and Mission education.

Living God, each of these tasks is vital to the ongoing work of
your Church; each involves many people. We give thanks for all
people involved in any way in these tasks. May they know the
guidance of your loving presence in all they do.

**In our life together fill us afresh, Lord God, that we might be
united in your love, held in your grace, empowered by your
Spirit.**

We pray for the spiritual and worship life of our church.
We remember:
> the work of local preachers
> the production of worship materials
> the use of drama, dance and music.

Living God, each of these tasks is vital to the ongoing work of
your Church; each involves many people. We give thanks for all
who encourage the spiritual and worship life of our church
communities. The Local Preachers of this circuit, those who
provide us with fresh resources and new ideas in dance, music,
drama, prayer and song. May each be filled with a fresh touch of
creativity and wonder as they continue to lead us.

**In our life together fill us afresh, Lord God, that we might be
united in your love, held in your grace, empowered by your
Spirit.**

Through Jesus Christ our Lord.
Amen.

CENTRAL SERVICES UNIT

Lord God, we know there is vital administrative work to be done by our church communities and we pray today for the work of the Unit for Service of the Methodist Church.

Lord God, refresh us all as we seek to serve you each day

We pray for the coordinating secretary of the Unit for Service (*name*). We thank you for the work s/he does on our behalf, and for his/her gifts and talents in administration. We ask that s/he will be constantly aware of your guiding and sustaining power in all s/he does, and find places of refreshment and recreation.

Lord God, refresh us all as we seek to serve you each day

We pray for the many individuals who work in our record and
archives departments,
those responsible for Connexional property
those who provide computer and secretarial knowledge
and skills.
Largely unknown by us we pray for them, that they will be continually refreshed and find fulfilment in the tasks that are theirs.

Lord God, refresh us all as we seek to serve you each day

We pray for the many individuals who work in communication:
for the publishing, production and distribution of resources
for the work of Epworth Press
for the work of the Methodist Publishing House
those who work on the publication of *Connect*, *Magnet*,
Epworth Review, the *Prayer Handbook*, *Worship and
Preaching* magazine and the *Partners in Learning* materials
for those who work in the Press Office.
Largely unknown by us we pray for them, that they will be continually refreshed and find fulfilment in the tasks that are theirs.

Lord God, refresh us all as we seek to serve you each day

We pray for the many individuals who work in finance:
  those responsible for budget preparation and for keeping accurate accounts
  those responsible for deciding on the payment of grants
  those responsible for the payment of stipends and pensions
  those responsible for managing investments
  the trustees for Methodist Church purposes
  those responsible for covenants.
Largely unknown by us we pray for them, that they will be continually refreshed and find fulfilment in the tasks that are theirs.

Lord God, refresh us all as we seek to serve you each day

We pray for the many individuals who work in Personnel:
  the Methodist ministers' housing society
  the minister retirement fund
  those responsible for lay employment
  the personnel office.
Largely unknown by us we pray for them, that they will be continually refreshed and find fulfilment in the tasks that are theirs.

Lord God, refresh us all as we seek to serve you each day

Lord God, there are so many hidden tasks, so many people we simply take for granted. Help us to be aware of the many ways in which we can serve you in the administrative tasks of your Church. We have such a rich diversity of resources in personnel, finance, talent, skill and knowledge; enable us to use those things as good stewards, putting the right resource in the right place at the right time.

Lord God, refresh us all as we seek to serve you each day

Lord God, hear our prayer, offered in the name of your Son, Jesus. **Amen.**

UNIT FOR INTER-CHURCH
AND OTHER RELATIONSHIPS

Almighty God, we acknowledge our place in a wider world.
A world of Christians who choose to worship you differently to us.
A world of other faiths, whose people choose a different belief
   system to us.
A world that can seem large, unfriendly, threatening
   and impersonal.
A world that can become smaller, less threatening and more
personal when we take time to learn about and understand
people who are different to us.
We pray for our relationships worldwide:
   our relationships with other Methodists in different cultures
   our relationships with other Christian groups
   our relationships with people of other faiths.

We pray for the Methodist Unit for Inter-Church and other
relationships and its work.
For the coordinating secretary, that s/he will have energy and
vision in making and building relationships. We ask that you will
equip him/her for this task with all that is needed to meet with
people of different faiths, cultures, beliefs and ideologies.

We pray for ecumenical relationships in all forms; local, national
and international.
   for the World Council of Churches
   the Conference of European churches
   the Council of Churches for Britain and Ireland
   Churches Together in Scotland
   Churches Together in Wales
   the Free Church Federal Council
   for Conversations with other churches
   for our local ecumenical projects.

Almighty God, in all our workings help us to find common
ground where communication and understanding is possible,
and not see only our differences. Help us to find a balance
between fearing and obliterating differences. Let us learn to
rejoice in difference and accept it as a strength, not a weakness.
Let us learn from those who are different to us, that we might
grow in our own faith and come to recognise the Christ in others.

Help us wherever possible to work with our neighbouring churches.

We pray for our relationships with those of other faiths.
Almighty God, give us wisdom, sensitivity and a willingness to understand the faith of others. We pray for those who are gifted in communicating with people of other faiths. May we learn from their experience and seek to work with people of faith in spite of our differences, finding a common bond in our humanity.
Help us wherever possible to work with our neighbours of other faiths.

We pray for World Church Relations and Mission Initiatives,
    for the sharing of resources
    for people serving overseas *(name any known)*
    the scholarship programme
    the youth exchange programme
    those responsible for making grants
    the World Methodist Council.

Almighty God, may these initiatives continue to help us
    in our mission.
Help us to grow in understanding and knowledge.
Help us to use what we have gained from these initiatives to learn more about the world in which we live.

Almighty God, we give you thanks for this world and its peoples.
Help us to become better informed about the world in which we live and enable us to grow in understanding of other faiths and cultures.

Through Jesus Christ our Lord.
Amen.

UNIT FOR CHURCH AND SOCIETY

Eternal God, you call us to be in the world but not of the world, and sometimes it is hard for us to find the right balance. We know we have a responsibility to be salt and light for society and we pray for this aspect of our Christian commitment.

Eternal God, this is our prayer and our desire, to serve you in serving others. Equip us for service, and motivate us to action.

We remember and pray for the coordinating secretary of the Unit for Church and Society (*name*). We give thanks for *him/her* and ask that *s/he* will be strengthened and renewed for service. May *s/he* know your abiding presence daily as *s/he* seeks to maintain present initiatives and explores new ways to proclaim your unchanging love in an ever-changing world.

Eternal God, this is our prayer and our desire, to serve you in serving others. Equip us for service, and motivate us to action.

We remember and pray for:
    chaplains to institutions, industry, places of education,
        prisons, hospitals and the armed forces
    those involved in the work of urban and rural mission
    those involved in the work of industrial mission
    the work of Luton Industrial College
    those engaged in sector ministry
    those in local broadcasting
    the work of Cliff College
    the work of the London Mission.

(*silence*)

Eternal God, there are so many initiatives seeking to bring a Christian perspective to life. Enable each person involved in these initiatives to shine with the light of Jesus, and find ways to share the gospel with love and sensitivity, in word and deed.

Eternal God, this is our prayer and our desire, to serve you in serving others. Equip us for service, and motivate us to action.

We remember and pray for:
  issues of public interest
  the issues surrounding our interpersonal and
      family relationships
  the work of NCH Action for Children
  the work of MHA
  political issues
  issues of racial justice
  issues of medical and professional ethics
  international issues
  the work of schools, colleges and universities
  the work of Southlands College
  the work of Westminster College.

(*silence*)

Eternal God, there are so many things of public interest that need our attention and prayers. We pray for those who are involved at the interface between church and society, that they may be strong and courageous, loving and giving.

Eternal God, this is our prayer and our desire, to serve you in serving others. Equip us for service, and motivate us to action.

Eternal God, we bring our prayers, knowing you long to hear us and knowing that we too can be involved in the answers. Equip us for service and motivate us to action. In the name of him who calls us out into the world, our Lord Jesus Christ. **Amen**.

CIRCUIT MEETING

Living God, we gather to discuss the business of this circuit. We come to find new ways to serve you and to keep a sense of vision before us. We come from our individual churches to share our resources, and to support each other in our continuing mission. We come to acknowledge your Lordship in our lives as individuals and as Church communities.

Living God, forgive us the times we stifle your Spirit,
forgive us the times we allow fear and apathy to blur our vision
forgive us the times we go our own way and ignore your guidance
Restore our vision.
Renew our strength and help us to walk in obedience
    to your calling.

Living God, we pray for the churches, small and large, that make up this circuit: the church we own as ours, the church that is near us, the churches that are distant from us. We pray for . . .

And we pray for the people who make these places living centres of worship.
Spirit of the Living God, fall afresh on each one.
Bring discernment, that we might know your way
bring love, that we might be clear channels of your love
bring courage, that we might stand firm, proclaiming your healing love in these places and situations.

Living God, we give you thanks, for you have carried us in our weakness, sustained us in our need and equipped us to follow.

Accept our prayers, offered in the name of Jesus and
    to your glory. **Amen.**

CHURCH COUNCIL

Almighty God, we gather to discuss the business of this church community.

We have practical matters to deal with:
    property and finance
    reports from various committees and working groups
    the appointment of people to various tasks within
        our community
    reports from Conference
    ecumenical relationships
    community relationships
    local, national and international affairs.
In all our discussions and decision-making guide us, Lord, to make good choices, that this community of faith may continue to live, work and grow.

We have spiritual matters to keep before us:
    the nature of the local church
    our worship life
    our mission
    our calling to be the light of Jesus in the world
    local, national and international needs.
In all our discussions and decision-making guide us, Lord; help us to keep a clear sense of your vision for us in the forefront of our minds, that this community of faith may grow in love and knowledge of Jesus.

We are different people with a common desire to serve you and see your kingdom grow:
    we have different needs
    we have different ideas about our worship and service
    we are all unique and we all need to be able to express
        our needs.
In all our discussions and decision-making help us, Lord, to listen to one another with openness, to respect the differences we represent and find ways of working with those differences, that we might be a community of faith that rejoices in variety, seeing it as a strength to be celebrated.

Almighty God, there is much work for us to do. Guide us, Lord, in all our thinking, speaking and decision-making that we might know your way and will for us.

In the name of Jesus we pray, and for his sake. **Amen.**

PASTORAL COMMITTEE

Heavenly Father, we commit this meeting to you, knowing that you are with us, leading us forward, guiding our decisions.

We thank you for those who are willing to serve this community as Class Leaders (*name them*)
We pray for them in their work and ask your blessing on them. Endow them with sensitivity and love as they fulfil this calling.

We thank you for those who are willing to serve this community as Stewards, (*name them*)
We pray for them in their work and ask your blessing on them. Endow them with vision and courage as they fulfil their calling.

As we review the membership of our church, help us to focus on the spiritual life of our community, finding ways to encourage people in their commitment to Christ. May we in this community recognise membership as a practical outworking of our commitment to you.

As we consider the life of this church, help us to focus on individual as well as community needs, finding ways to encourage people in their faith by offering support, prayer and practical help.

As we seek for ways to move forward as a community, help us to focus our strengths and energies, that we might offer training where needed as people take up jobs within our church.

Heavenly Father, as we meet,
bless us that we might be a blessing to others,
refresh us that we might be renewed for service.
In Jesus' name we pray.
Amen.

FAREWELL SERVICE

Praise:

Come, let us bless the Lord and praise him for ever.
Holy God, we worship you and magnify your name.

Come, let us bless the Lord and praise his name

Praise him for his majesty and power
Praise him for his love and mercy
Praise him for his faithfulness and steadfastness.

Come, let us bless the Lord and praise his name

Praise him with our hearts and minds
Praise him with our will and emotions
Praise him with our whole being.

Come, let us bless the Lord and praise his name

Praise him for his creativity
Praise him for sending his Son Jesus to be our Saviour
Praise him for the gift of the Holy Spirit in our lives.

Come, let us bless the Lord and praise his name

Holy God, we worship you and magnify your name today and always through Jesus Christ our Lord. **Amen.**

Confession:

Come, let us confess our sins to God,
knowing he will always forgive those who are truly sorry.
Holy God, we acknowledge our sins

(*silence*)

we seek your forgiveness
we ask for your strength to resist temptation.
Forgive us, Holy Lord,
for all that we have done that we should not have done

(*silence*)

and for all that we have failed to do

(*silence*)

Renew us, Holy Lord,
for we ask in the name of Jesus, our Lord and Saviour. **Amen.**

Intercessions:

Brothers and Sisters in Christ, we join together in prayer and bring our requests to the Father, knowing that he hears us.

Heavenly Father, in times of transition we need the security of your presence. We are a pilgrim people, moving through endings and into new beginnings. Help us as we negotiate an ending and look toward a new beginning.

We rejoice in and give thanks for the minister*(s)* (*named*) who have served in these churches (*named*) and this circuit. We give thanks for *his/her/their* life, work and witness among us and for the many ways in which we have grown in faith together.

Lord God, you understand us better than we do ourselves.
You know the mixed feelings we have as we remember
    the good times and the not so good times,
    the times of great blessing and the times of sheer hard work
    and frustration with each other.
We know that all those things come about because we have strengths and weaknesses, we are human and limited.

In spite of the ups and downs of our life together, we are grateful for the opportunities we have had to journey in faith, and we ask you to bless us and these ministers as we each move on to new things.

We pray for:
    the people of this circuit,
    the people of *this church/these churches* (*named*)
    this/these minister*(s)*, and *his/her/their* family*(ies)*.

Lord God, you understand that change is hard for us
    to negotiate;
we like everything to be safe and secure, familiar and known.
Lord, take our fears and transform them with your courage.
Lord, take our worries and transform them with your grace.
Lord, take our anxieties and transform them with your love.
Lord, take our sadness and transform it in Jesus, through your Holy Spirit.

Heavenly Father, our life with you is a journey, a journey of faith, trust and hope. You transform our lives and ask us to move on with you. You promise your courage, grace, love and Spirit and we rely on your promises. Lord, accept our commitment made afresh this day, that we will be your people and travel with you into a new beginning.

Through Jesus Christ our Lord.
Amen.

WELCOME SERVICE

Collect:

Almighty God, as your Son, Jesus, called those first disciples, so we too have been called into your service. As we worship, enable each of us to know your way for us, and give us courage to follow where you lead.

Through Jesus Christ our Lord. **Amen**.

Praise:

Giving Father, you are worthy of our praise and adoration
You are the one whom we seek with all our heart
You are the one whom we extol
You are the one who gives meaning and sense to our lives
You are the one whom we worship and adore.

Living Lord Jesus, you are worthy of our praise and adoration
You are the one whom we seek with all our heart
You are the one whom we extol
You are the one who showed us the way of love
You are the one whom we worship and adore.

Loving Holy Spirit, you are worthy of our praise and adoration
You are the one whom we seek with all our heart
You are the one whom we extol
You are the one who guides and comforts
You are the one whom we worship and adore.

Eternal God, Father, Son and Holy Spirit, you are worthy of our praise and adoration.
You are the one whom we seek, you are the one whom we extol.
Prompted by your Holy Spirit and in the name of Jesus
we honour you with our praise and adoration.
Amen.

Confession:

Eternal God, forgive our sins.
We know things with our heads and yet so often we do not grasp them with our hearts.
We say we understand your call and believe you will equip us, and yet so often we do not trust in your way and will for us.

We try to do so many things in our own strength. We show by our actions that we think we know best.
Eternal God, forgive us:
  draw close to us
  renew our spirits
  and forgive our transgressions
for we ask it in the name of your precious Son, Jesus Christ.
Amen.

Intercessions:

Lord God, you call us to journey with you into new situations and unknown places. You promise your presence and provision as we walk your way.

Lord, you have called us to walk in faith:
Renew us for the journey

We pray for the Methodist circuit in this place:
  That we will journey with courage, and a willingness to
    work together.
  That we will continually seek God's blessing and power in all
    our endeavours.
  That we will be a people of vision.

Lord, you have called us to walk in faith:
Renew us for the journey

We pray for the churches receiving a new minister:
  That they will journey with trust and a willingness to be
    dependent on God.
  That they will continually seek God's blessing and power in
    their endeavours.
  That they will be a people of faith.

Lord, you have called us to walk in faith:
Renew us for the journey

We pray for the minister (*name*) called to serve here:
  That *s/he* will journey with hope and an assurance of God's
    presence daily.
  That *s/he* will continually seek God's blessing and power in
    his/her endeavours.
  The *s/he* will be a person of hope

Lord, you have called us to walk in faith:
Renew us for the journey

We pray for *his/her* family
  That they will journey with patience and stamina.
  That they will continually know God's blessing and power in
    all their endeavours.
  That they will be a people of trust.

Lord, you have called us to walk in faith:
Renew us for the journey

Lord, you have called us to journey with you
You have promised to provide for our needs
We go forward into an unknown future, certain of your guiding hand, aware of your presence, and trusting in you for all that may come
In the name of him who trusted himself completely to your will, our Lord Jesus Christ.
Amen.

CHURCH ANNIVERSARY

Confession:

Almighty God, on this anniversary day we acknowledge before you the thoughtlessness of so many of our actions.
We have been greedy
We have been selfish
We have been self-centred
We have been self-absorbed
We have fallen again and again.
Our experience tells us that with you there is always the possibility of new beginnings.
Forgive us; help us to follow you more closely and find new ways to serve you in this place.
Through Jesus Christ our Lord. **Amen**.

Praise and Thanksgiving:

Almighty God, we give you thanks and praise.
For sending your Son to redeem us
For sending your Spirit to renew us
For calling us to be your people
For your presence in our lives
For sustaining us in this place.

Almighty God, we give you thanks and praise

For this building and its witness
For those who have worshipped here throughout the years
for those who have given us our traditions of service and worship
For those who have passed on your word to us
For those who have stretched us in our faith.

Almighty God, we give you thanks and praise.

For sending your Son to restore us
For sending your Spirit to challenge us
For calling us to follow you
For your grace in our lives
For continuing to guide us in this place.

Almighty God, we give you thanks and praise

For the life of this church
For those who serve you here
For those who have remained faithful to your call
    over many years
For those who have encouraged us in our Christian walk
For those who are new to faith.
Almighty God, we give you thanks and praise

Glory and honour and power are yours, Almighty God
We rejoice on this anniversary day;
we give you thanks and praise.
Through Jesus Christ our Lord. **Amen**.

Intercessions:

Almighty God, on this anniversary day we thank you for this building and for the prayers and worship that have been offered here. We pray that you will enable us to continue to make this place a centre of worship and service to you. May we always shine with the light of Jesus, serve this community and draw others into our fellowship.

Almighty God, on this anniversary day we pray for the worship life of this church. May we honour the traditions of those who have gone before. May we continue to find new ways to worship you as you deserve. May we learn to offer ourselves afresh to the moving of your Spirit. May we be a centre of living worship to the living God.

Almighty God, on this anniversary day we pray for the life of this church and for all who serve this community. Our minister, church stewards, Junior Church teachers, cleaners, stewards of property, our treasurer, all who serve on committees, and all who lead various groups, the Ladies meeting, the Guild, the mothers-and-toddlers and the Bible study group. May we all continue to grow in grace and acknowledge your Lordship in our lives.

Almighty God, on this anniversary day we pray for the mission of this church. May we be so united in love and friendship that others will see something attractive and magnetic, something of value in this place and want to be a part of our church.

Almighty God, on this anniversary day we pray for the outreach of this church. May we find courage to reach out to the community beyond these walls. Help us to be involved with our will and our actions.

Almighty God, on this anniversary day we pray for all who have been baptised and all who have been married here. May they and their families come to know your love and grace and turn to you in times of need.

Almighty God, on this anniversary day we thank you for the men and women who have worshipped and served you throughout the generations in this place. We pray that we may be as faithful in worship and service, that future generations may continue to worship and serve you here.

Almighty God, on this anniversary day we thank you for all that is past, and place our trust in you for the future. Renew our vision and help us to look to the future with hope, acknowledging your Lordship in our lives.

Through Jesus Christ our Lord.
Amen.

FOR CHILDREN

Intercessions:

We pray for the children of our church:
  children of our church families.
  children sent because it is thought good for them.
  children who make their own way here.
  children baptised here, for whom we have made promises.

Lord, this is our prayer: help us to know and to do your will

Lord, help us to remember that our church is their church.
Through the power of your Holy Spirit may our church be a place
of love and acceptance, joy and revelation for our children.

Lord, this is our prayer: help us to know and to do your will

We pray for all children who suffer in any way:
  for the sick and handicapped
  for the hungry and disadvantaged
  for the bereaved and refugee
Lord, loving parent of all, comfort your suffering children.

Lord, this is our prayer: help us to know and to do your will

We ask you to forgive us, Lord:
  for children unloved, neglected or abused
  for children torn apart by the break up of marriages
  for children lonely and teased because they are different
  for children burdened with responsibilities they are too
    young to take.
Loving parent of all, nurture your children.

Lord, this is our prayer: help us to know and to do your will

In you, Father, we are one family. We give thanks for children.
We thank you for the newness, imagination, trustfulness and
energy they possess. We thank you for children we know and
have known, and for what they have taught us about you. Help
us to follow your example in Jesus and bring all your children,
young and old, into the fullness of your love.

Through Jesus Christ our Lord. **Amen**.

125

NCH ACTION FOR CHILDREN

Our prayers today are for the work of NCH Action for Children, begun in 1869 by Rev Thomas Stephenson. Over the years NCH has changed and grown in a continued effort to meet the changing needs of society's children. They have always sought to put the needs of children first, ensuring that the public has been aware of the rapidly changing place of children in our world. As well as the work in this country, NCH Action for Children also supports a number of childcare and training projects overseas.

Intercessions:

Heavenly Father, we thank you for the work of NCH Action for Children and we pray for its continued service. We thank you for the men and women who work in the various projects, putting the needs of children first, making us aware of their needs and how we can help.

We remember and pray for the work of the:
Family and Community Centres
community-based projects for young offenders
services for children with disabilities
Leaving Care/homeless projects
child sexual abuse treatment centres.
counselling services
residential homes/schools
Homefinding services.

We pray for those who work in them, the project leaders, the helpers, all who give of themselves to support children and their families, in whatever capacity. Continually refresh them for their work and give them a sense of joy and satisfaction in what they do.
We pray for the children, young people and families who need these centres, that they will know themselves to be important and valued, that they will find healing for their hurts and hope for the future.

We remember and pray for the work of:
   the Central Office, London
   the many support staff
   the Directors of Advocacy, Finance and Administration,
   Policy and Information, the Pastoral Director and the
   Assistant Director of Operations
   the nine regional Directors of Social Work.

We pray for each one of them that they will continue to be advocates for children, and be courageous and strong as they seek for new initiatives in meeting the many needs of our children.

We remember and pray for the work of fund raising, the:
   house-to-house collections
   school projects envelopes
   church and community projects
   companies and trusts.

We give thanks for the money raised and pray that all of us will continue to believe in the importance of this work and raise much needed finance, so that child poverty, child hunger, child crime and child homelessness will become things of the past.

Heavenly Father, we know that your word tells us that we must become like children to inherit your kingdom. We thank you for the children we have known who have shared themselves with us and given us a glimpse of childlike trust and faith. Motivate us to work for children, ensuring that they have places of safety and nurture in which to grow.

In the Name of Jesus, our Lord and Saviour, we pray.
Amen.

METHODIST HOMES

Almighty God, we remember today the work of Methodist Homes.

We pray for those who work in the head office in Derby
We remember those responsible for publicity
the raising of much needed finance
the pastoral care of staff and residents
and those responsible for allocating places of residence to elderly people in need.
May all those involved in the work at head office fulfil their duties well and know peace in serving you in this work.

We pray for the residential homes, the sheltered housing projects and the live-at-home schemes around the country. May all residents in these places feel truly at home.
We pray that these initiatives will continue to meet the physical, emotional and spiritual needs of people as they grow older and less able to live independently.

We pray for those who staff the various projects in whatever capacity,
We remember the work of:
    carers
    caterers
    gardeners
    cleaners
    and chaplains.
May they find satisfaction in their work, be channels of your grace and know your presence in their daily tasks.

We pray for the elderly people in this community:
    for those no longer able to attend worship due to infirmity
    for those who feel lonely
    for those who feel abandoned by family
    for those afraid of a future of increasing dependence.
We pray that they will know your comforting presence.
And we pray that we will be a community that values the contribution of all among us.

Almighty God, we thank you for the work of Methodist Homes and pray that it will continue to meet the needs of elderly people for generations to come. In Jesus' name we pray. **Amen**.

AMNESTY INTERNATIONAL

Amnesty International is a voluntary organisation with a worldwide membership. It seeks to release prisoners of conscience, irrespective of their political ideology, ethnic origin, sex, or religious belief. A prisoner of conscience is defined as anyone who is imprisoned or detained because of consciously held belief, and who has not used or advocated violence.

(Can include prayers for specific prisoners of conscience known to individuals through Amnesty International or the pages of the Methodist Recorder.)

Intercessions:

Lord God, we admit our ignorance about what happens to people in other countries. Individuals are held in prison, tortured and killed for their beliefs or because of their race, religion or gender. And we remain unaware, or only vaguely aware, of what happens in secret. Lord God, help us to become aware of what happens in oppressive regimes, when people are not free to hold their own beliefs, but must subscribe to the ruling political ideology.

We thank you for the freedom we enjoy and pray for courage to use that freedom well, and not turn away from those in need.

Lord God, we pray for the work of Amnesty International, for the men and women who work hard to change situations of torture and detainment without a fair trial. For those who bring us information so that we can help. We pray for them that they will be sustained in the task, and use whatever non-violent means are available in their struggle for justice for all people.

Lord God, we pray for governments and leaders who violate human rights, using torture, imprisonment and death, who rule by fear and might and power. We pray for a change of heart, an understanding of the immorality of such action. We pray that individuals will have enough courage to say 'no' and change such situations.

Lord God, we pray for men and women who are at present being held without trial, because of race, colour or creed. We pray that those who are tortured, and those who are injured in body, mind and spirit will find an inner strength that will help them rise above the actions of those who hold the power.

Lord God, we pray for families who do not know where a loved one is, or who know that a loved one is imprisoned or being tortured, and who can seemingly do little to help. We pray that they will find strength and courage to live with uncertainty, and find ways to challenge what has happened to them and their families.

Lord God, we pray you to accept our prayers in the name of him who died for our freedom, our Lord Jesus Christ. **Amen**.

SAMARITANS

Intercessions:

Heavenly Father, we remember today the work of the Samaritans.

We remember before you all who work as volunteers.
The men and women who have trained, and who give up their time to listen to the needs of others. We pray for them.
We give thanks for the work they do, and ask that they will be sustained and supported.

We remember before you the trainers.
The men and women who use their knowledge and skills to enable others to take on this work.
The men and women in training, who are learning about themselves and how to help others. We pray for them.
We give thanks for trainers and trainees and ask that they will share their skills and knowledge and so be effective listeners.

We remember before you the financial needs of the Samaritans.
We give thanks for those who give financial support.
For those who hold fund raising events, the local authorities who give grants and the companies which give donations.
We pray that funds will continue to be available and that the money will be used wisely and to good effect.

We remember before you the outreach programme.
The men and women who work to build awareness of the work of Samaritans among groups of people who are a high suicide risk.
For the work with prisoners, the elderly, the young, and rural and ethnic communities.
We give thanks for this work, and ask that the outreach programme will be effective in educating and reaching those high risk groups.

We remember before you that this work is about people, people in need.
We pray for people who need a listening ear
    to talk about their loneliness
    to talk about their difficulties
    to share their pains and struggles with life.

We give thanks for their courage in seeking help and ask that they be met with understanding and encouragement.

Heavenly Father, we bring our prayers in the name of the one who is always willing to listen to us, our Lord and Saviour, Jesus Christ. **Amen**.

COMPASSIONATE FRIENDS

Compassionate Friends is a self-help organisation that helps parents whose children have died. It also supports and befriends siblings and grand-parents.

Intercessions:

Heavenly Father, we pray today for the work of Compassionate Friends, and for parents grieving the loss of a child.

We pray for those who work in the central office, Bristol; for the full-time administrator and for the support staff. We thank you for their work, and for the help and support they give to parents and families in distress. We pray that they may be strengthened for their work, and find a sense of fulfilment in supporting people in need. We pray that they too will find support for their stresses and pains.

Lord of compassion, this is our prayer; hear us

We pray for the funding needed to keep this essential work operating, that grants and donations will be forthcoming from various agencies, both government and voluntary. We pray that we will be open hearted and generous in our support of this work.

Lord of compassion, this is our prayer; hear us

We pray for all the groups that comprise this organisation, both here and abroad. We pray for the national committee, the Annual General Meeting and the local groups, that in the sharing of their stories parents can support and help each other. We pray that the talks, the discussions and group meetings may be times of healing as people adjust to life without their child.

Lord of compassion, this is our prayer; hear us

We pray that the leaflets, quarterly newsletters, journals and videos may continue to help parents in their search for understanding and support. We pray for the groups within Compassionate Friends which deal with specific situations: Parents of Murdered Children (PoMC); Shadow of Suicide, for those whose child had died through suicide, and SIBBS, Support in Bereavement for Brothers and Sisters. We pray that these groups will be able to address the particular difficulties those situations raise.

Lord of compassion, this is our prayer; hear us

We pray for those parents whose children have died, that there will be places where they can express their complex feelings, share their loss and bewilderment and find a listening ear and a supportive hand. Help us to be people who can share their pain, and journey with them through the wilderness to a place of hope.

Lord of compassion, this is our prayer; hear us

We pray for parents who are angry, confused and struggling to come to terms with their loss. For those who blame themselves, those who blame others, those who blame you, Lord God. We pray that they will find ways to grieve and heal, and we pray that people will stay with them in their anger and despair, however long it takes. We pray that they will find peace.

Lord of compassion, this is our prayer; hear us

Heavenly Father, Lord of compassion, we bring these our prayers to you, knowing that you understand the pain and heartache of loss.

We offer them in the name of Jesus our Compassionate Friend and Saviour. **Amen**.

RELATE

God of love, we remember and pray today for the work of Relate.

Relationships are such a mixed blessing; they bring joy beyond our wildest imagining, great happiness, and a sense of peace. But they also bring stress, strain and unhappiness. It is hard for us to comprehend how something so good can also be so bad. How can that which is designed to bring such joy also bring misery?

We expect our relationships to be good; we invest a great deal of time and emotional energy in them, and we want them to be good always. But sometimes our expectations are unrealistic, and we are disappointed when our intimate relationships do not live up to the fairy tale image we have of them. Help us to bear with that disappointment, to realise that nothing can be perfect all the time, and accept that we are all human and we all have our failings.

When things do go badly wrong, it is good to know that there are places and people to whom we can go for help and support.
Today we thank you for the work of Relate, for those people who give of themselves and their time to help couples work through difficult and painful times.
We pray for those who are trained to help, and we thank you for their skills and their patience.
We pray for those who train others to help and support couples in crisis.
God of love, keep them focused on this important work, and enable them to be supportive and non-judgmental.

We pray for couples in crisis, facing difficult and distressing times, and needing guidance from an outside source. Help them to be honest in their seeking, that they may find a way forward from this place of pain. Enable them to live with the decisions they make, that they may discover new strength in their relationships.
God of love, keep them focused on this important work and enable them to see growth and change.

We pray for couples who will decide that separation is the right thing for them. May they be supported in the process of

separation, learn to mourn what is lost, deal with the feelings of failure and find some sense of hope for the future.
God of love, keep them focused and enable them to know the love and support of family and friends.

We pray for the individuals who spend so much time listening to the struggles of couples, that they might be supported in this valuable work, and not become overwhelmed by negative emotions.
God of love, keep them focused and enable them to find joy in this task.

We pray for resources, that the work of Relate may continue. For people skilled to train others for the work. For people willing to be trained, and for funds to be made available by those who control the purse strings.
God of love, we bring our prayers in the name of him who is love, our Lord Jesus.
Amen.

Blessings

1.

May God the Father bless you.
May Jesus the Son continually redeem you.
May the Holy Spirit refresh you
as you serve God in the world.
Go in peace, God goes with you.
Amen.

2.

May God bless us and keep us in his care
as we go from this place, renewed and restored.
The Lord be with us all, today and forever.
Amen.

3.

Light of the world, coming to dispel our darkness,
Burn forever in our hearts, an inextinguishable flame.
Shine on in us, that we might shine with your love
in the dark places of our world.
Amen.

4.

God, who calls men and women to follow,
enlarge our vision of you, let your Spirit
move through us, filling us with light and life.
Make us clear channels of your love and grace
that we might serve you in serving others.
Jesus, the light of the world goes with us.
Amen.

5.

God of life, as we go from this place of worship
give us the courage to take seriously the task of
    following you.
Fill us with the strength to dare to believe in your
    purposes for us.
The Father, the Son and the Holy Spirit bless you and
    be in you, today and always.
Amen.

INDEX